CRICUT MAKER & CRICUT EXPLORER AIR 2

The Updated Guide For Beginners To Set Up Cricut Explorer Air 2 and Cricut Maker. Step By Step Instructions, Tricks And Tools To Create Your Project Ideas From Zero In An Easy Way.

MIKE DAWSON

CONTENTS

CRICUT MAKER GUIDE FOR BEGINNERS

CRICUT EXPLORE AIR 2

CHAPTER 1: WHAT IS CRICUT MACHINE

CHAPTER 2: MACHINE SETUP AND HOW TO PREPARE THE MATERIAL

CHAPTER 3: CRICUT DESIGN SPACE SOFTWARE FOR CRICUT EXPLORE AIR 2

CHAPTER 4: SOLVING THE MOST COMMON PROBLEM WHEN USING CRICUT EXPLORE AIR 2

Copyright

CRICUT MAKER GUIDE FOR BEGINNERS

The Comprehensive Guide For Beginners To Master The Cricut Maker, Its Accessories & Materials. How to cut and produce beautiful DIY projects and crafts

Introduction

Okay, you've bought a Cricut machine, and you are excited. You have thought so much on what you are going to do with it. Now you have it. You really don't know the process. Well, that is why I am here. We would talk extensively about Cricut project ideas.

Whatever you have in mind, maybe you want to become this craftsperson, or you just want to do it for fun in a school or office we have several ideas for you here

You can buy these machines from an online store or at a craft store. And the price would definitely depend upon the model you choose. Furthermore, the prince can range anywhere from $100-$350 (and above), so it is better you narrow down your needs and go for it. Whatever makes your work more comfortable and efficient can be regarded as a significant investment. The Cricut is one of them; it is rewarding and fun to use. Anyone can benefit from it. Because of its efficiency, we have Cricut in places we never envisioned that they would be in previous years.

We have Cricut in offices and workshops. Does that sound strange to you? It shouldn't be because Cricut is never meant to be a home-only tool. It is time-saving and makes your work so professional, and the beautiful thing about it is that there are no limits to it, you can do whatever you can. If you're reading this book, then you have a Cricut machine in your possession, and maybe you don't really know how to use it. Well, I am here to help you with that.

First, we have the Cricut maker which is a machine used with design space. This Cricut maker has a cloud-based online software. And this particular series or design cannot function alone you would need to use the design space on a desktop or a laptop computing, and of course, internet connection is needed.

Another special provision provided with the Cricut maker is that you can make use of the offline feature in the design space app whenever you're using the design app on an IOS device, i.e., an iPad/iPhone or MacBook. This means you can make designs and all without an internet connection. This is just one device, and that is not all because each device has its own peculiarities added to the general feature that we all know. We also have the Cricut Explore Air.

This invention of Robert Workman with the collaboration of fellow investors like Jonathan Johnson, Matt Strong, and Phil Beffrey is also pronounced as cricket. This product has been able to gather so many revenues in sales within a short period of time because of its effectiveness and handiness.

This machine has been in work for years, and it totally blows everyone's mind and any other cutting machine out there. They keep bringing more and more to the table, and they keep adding something new every now and then. The Cricut has been able to dominate that market because of its reliability, performance, durability and its firmware also. This force of paper crafting revolution can also work without being connected or hooked to a computer. There are some designs that are portable and convenient to carry. Are you thinking of creating an endless assortment of shapes, letters, and phrases? Don't think too far, just get a Cricut.

How to choose the right machine for your needs

On the whole, your choice of model depends on the type of use you will be giving it. This is the main criteria to take into consideration. If you are a casual hobbyist, then you might want to get the basic model. This will allow you to avoid spending more than you'd like while getting all of the benefits from the Cricut Machine. If you are planning on using it for business purposes, then it might be best to consider getting the top of the line model.

With that in mind, let's take a look at the criteria that we can take into consideration when purchasing a Cricut Machine. So, your answer to the following questions will help you make a decision on which model is the most suitable for you.

CRITERIA FOR CHOOSING A CRICUT MACHINE

Here are five questions that you ought to ask yourself when looking to purchase your first Cricut Machine. Be honest as the answers to these questions will reveal the right model for you. That way, you can get the most out of your Cricut Machine without breaking the bank.

. . .

WHAT AM I GOING TO USE IT FOR?

If you are a casual hobbyist and crafter, that is, you don't plan to use the machine heavily, the Explore Air model would suit you just fine. This model offers all of the capabilities that the other models offer though it isn't quite as robust as the others. This is perfect if you don't plan to use it heavily, such as cutting a large number of items in one go. It's perfect if you are looking to cut one or two items at a time.

On the other hand, if you are looking to make heavy use of the machine, such as in the case of business use, then the Cricut Maker may be the best option for you. While it's the priciest, it's also the fastest and most robust of the lot. Given the fact that it's the most powerful model, you'll be able to cut anything and produce a large number of items in a short time.

HOW MUCH AM I WILLING TO SPEND ON A CRICUT MACHINE?

On the other hand, if you are looking for a more budget-friendly solution, then the Explore Air makes the most sense. As we have stated earlier, if you are looking to avoid spending a great deal of money, then you can even pick up a used one. Since the Cricut Machine is pretty solid, you won't have to worry about it being in bad shape. Of course, it depends on how it was treated by its previous owner. But on the whole, they are usually in pretty good shape, especially if it doesn't have a lot of mileage on it.

If you are looking to purchase it for business purposes, then you might want to consider the Cricut Maker. It offers all of the features you need and will handle any workload you throw its way. While any of the other models will do the trick, the Maker is by far the fastest machine. In the world of business, time is certainly an important consideration. So, it only makes sense to get the fastest machine available to you.

SHOULD I UPGRADE MY CRICUT MACHINE?

Assuming you have already taken the plunge with your first Cricut

Machine, you might consider upgrading your current model. This is especially true if the breadth and scope of your projects have outgrown your current machine.

A note of caution though: if you are looking for serious power, then getting the Maker is the best way to go. However, it isn't recommended to get it used, at least not if you're looking to upgrade for serious use. The reason for this is that the Maker is a powerful machine, but it may be put through the wringer. So, getting a brand-new makes sense if you're considering putting some serious mileage on it. Alternatively, the Joy can be a great upgrade, particularly if you something smaller to work with.

What add-ons can I get with the Cricut Machine?

When you get a Cricut Machine, you get access to any number of add-ons and tools which can be used to make any number of creations. These add-ons consist of pens, cartridges, and other tools that can be used to make effects beyond the standard cutting function. Cricut has gone a long way toward making a vast array of tools available. That's something that can't be said about other similar kinds of machines on the market.

It is worth paying close attention to the chapter in which we will discuss the types of tools available to you. That way, you can see for yourself just how many options you have available. In the end, the Cricut Machine offers the best balance in terms of capability and function. You can create plenty of designs while working with several techniques. When you put it all together, the overall capabilities of the Cricut Machine place it at the top of its category.

Quick Overview of the Main Models

The Cricut Machine is one of the most sophisticated tools that can be used in the world of arts and crafts. It allows you to make a myriad of creations by combining its specially designed software and then translate it into a physical form of art.

In essence, the Cricut Machine is a cutting machine. It can cut any number of materials based on predetermined patterns that you develop in the specially designed software. In these creations, you can take a material, and have the Cricut Machine cut out the patterns you want it to.

Now, it should be noted that this device is meant to cut only. It doesn't do any printing. So, that's an important thing to keep in mind. For instance, you can cut out an elaborate design on a piece of leather and then color it to your liking. If you are making a birthday card, you can cut out the design you like and then color it using your technique of choice (pastels, crayons, paints, watercolors, and so on).

That being said, the Cricut Machine is a great tool for any type of project. You can go as elaborate as you like. The important thing is to make sure you have the right idea in mind. Based on that, you can make anything work for you.

CRICUT MAKER

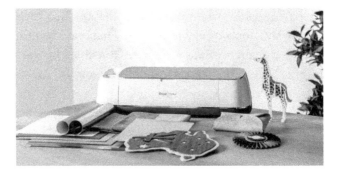

THE CRICUT MAKER IS THE FIRST AND ONLY DEVICE FROM CRICUT that can be used with a Rotary blade to cut fabrics directly. It is also equipped with a scoring wheel that can exert varying pressure to allow scoring of thicker papers. It provides the most diverse variety of tools to cut, score, write, and even decorate; so you can truly bring your dream projects to life. Moreover, the company is looking to add even more tools that can be used with Cricut Maker and quickly switched to support your creative growth continually.

With the versatile housing slot, you can just press the "quick release" button on the device to mount any desired tip and kick start your craft project.

Features:

- Fast and precision cut creating a rotary blade.
- Use the knife blade to cut thin as well as thick materials.
- Use 12 x 12 inches cutting mats with fine point pen.
- It offers a number of digital sewing patterns.
- Use your own designs.
- It comes with a device docking slot.
- Equipped with Bluetooth wireless technology.
- A USB port allows charging your mobile devices while in use.

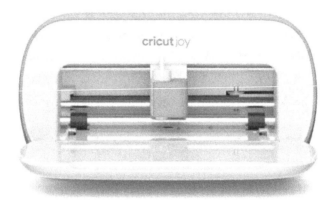

CRICUT JOY

It's the most up to date machine Cricut discharged. It's very small and it can cut, draw a wide assortment of materials. the Cricut Joy can cut and remove vinyl and iron-on without a tangle!

You may have the option to buy them on amazon or utilized. In any case, they are not good with Cricut Design Space and the product they used previously – Cricut Craft Room – has been closed down totally. Composing with your Cricut is so natural and fun. It's an extraordinary method to give an undertaking proficient introduction with an individual and custom made feel.

On the off chance that you sew a great deal it might simply be justified, despite all the trouble to have that rotating shaper. Also, how cool is it to have wood patterns? Words cut in wood are overly popular at this moment. Furthermore, who realizes what number of more apparatuses Cricut will come out with that will just work in the Maker.

CRICUT COMPARE MODELS

Cricut is exploring one, Cricut Explore Aire, Cricut, and Cricut Explore Air 2 Maker.

With these options, you might be wondering what the differences between them are and what to buy.

I will explore these models and then briefly explain the Cricut machines should be used depending on the depth on the ship.

CUTTING FORCE

The machine comes with a carbide blade premium German first category, which can be cut through thick materials and light equally clearly and cleanly form. Even if exploring one is recommended for beginners, it is very professional. The blade is also very durable.

As for the width of cutting, explore one can cut sizes ranging from 23

½ "high and ¼ to ½" 11 wide.

Although the explore one looks excellent, there are some activities that can be done in the design space Cricut if you are using this model.

Cricut Design Space is very user-friendly when used to explore one. It accepts .jpg, .png, and .bmp.

In addition, the Cricut Explore One cannot work wirelessly. To add comfort to it and does not care about the cost, then you can buy a Bluetooth adapter and use it to transfer images or files wirelessly.

EXPLORE CRICUT AIR

While this is quite similar to the Explore One model, which also comes with some additional features, the main difference between them is the presence of the built-in Bluetooth adapter. If you enjoy seeing no cables and wires around your workplace, especially with the risk of tripping over them, then this model solves that problem.

CAPACITY

Explore air is also exploring different ones as it has a double carriage. This means that you can draw, write, or record while mowing because it has two clamps to hold both tools. This saves you money because you do not have to buy an adapter tool.

MATERIALS

Explore air is quite liberating when it comes to materials. It features a dial that can allow you to choose the material you are about to cut. This way, you do not have to guess the depth of the blade and spoil the material.

The machine will know how deeply felt the need to cut and what kind you have to be paper or vinyl. This is especially great for beginners' feature that they are not well versed in the depths of the sheet.

DIFFERENCE IN MODELS

In general, there is no difference between the three models of Cricut Machine. They are all capable of cutting out the same types of patterns and materials. As such, may casual hobbyists would instead go for the Joy (especially when looking affordability and portability) or the Explore Air (especially when looking for an excellent entry-level product). However, it's the Maker that shines when it comes to using all of the tools available. By using the Maker, you have the opportunity to unlock the power of the Cricut Machine. It can cut through thicker and stricter material while allowing you the versatility of the various tools we outlined in the previous chapter.

If you are seriously considering the Cricut Machine for heavy-duty crafting or business purposes, then the Maker makes the most sense. After all, it will provide you with the best all-around features and value. Sure, the price is the highest, but in the end, the large array of projects you will be able to carry out will may the machine worth the investment.

Additionally, you will find that the size of the materials will vary between the Joy and Explore Air/Maker. Given the fact that the Joy is much smaller, you are only able to cut materials roughly half the size of the other two machines. This is something which you need to keep in mind if you are considering the Joy. Otherwise, any of the three models will provide you with excellent results.

Cricut Maker

Machine Setup and How to Prepare the Material

First, you'll want to set up the Cricut Joy. To begin, create a space for it. A craft room is the best place for this, but if you're at a loss of where to put it, I suggest setting it up in a dining room if possible. Make sure you have an outlet nearby or a reliable extension cord.

Next, read the instructions. Often, you can jump right in and begin using the equipment, but with Cricut machines, it can be very tedious.

Make sure that you do have ample free space around the machine itself, because you will be loading mats in and out and you'll need that little bit of wiggle room.

The next thing to set up is, of course, the computer where the designs will be created. Make sure that whatever medium you're using has an internet connection, since you'll need to download the Cricut Design Space app. If it's a machine earlier than the Explore Air 2, it will need to be plugged in directly, but if it's a wireless machine like the Air 2, you can simply link this up to your computer, and from there, design what you need to design.

. . .

IMPUTING CARTRIDGES AND KEYPAD

The first cut that you'll be doing does involve keypad input and cartridges, and these are usually done with the "Enjoy Card" project you get right away. So, once everything is set up, choose this project, and from there, you can use the tools and the accessories within the project.

You will need to set the smart dial before you get started making your projects. This is on the right side of the Explore Air 2, and it's basically the way you choose your materials. Turn the dial to whatever type of material you want, since this does help with ensuring you've got the right blade settings. There are even half settings for those in-between projects.

For example, let's say you have some light cardstock. You can choose that setting, or the adjacent half setting. Once this is selected in Design Space, your machine will automatically adjust to the correct location.

You can also choose the fast mode, which is in the "set, load, go" area on the screen, and you can then check the position of the box under the indicator for dial position. Then, press this and make your cut. However, fast mode is incredibly loud, so be careful.

Once it's confirmed, you can go to images, and click the cartridges option to find the ones that you want to make. You can filter the cartridges to figure out what you need, and you can check out your images tab for any other cartridges that are purchased or uploaded.

You can get digital cartridges, which means you buy them online and choose the images directly from your available options. They aren't physical, so there is no linking required.

CARTRIDGE

Cartridges are expensive, they truly are, but they are so easy and fun to use as well. Cartridges contain a huge amount of images and fonts. They are all themed so they can be purchased according to what you need them for. Some cartridges only contain letters, and these have really cool fonts that can be used to write on cards or cut with your machine. Each one of them also has a fair amount of options that will allow you to customize the design as much as you want.

You will need to link the cartridge of the new machines to the Design Space; hence, an internet connection is necessary if you wish to work with them within the application itself. The older machines do not have such a requirement, but the upgraded ones do. So, either way, you will need an internet connection for linking the cartridges or setting up with Design Space.

LOADING YOUR PAPER

To load paper into a Cricut machine, you'll want to make sure that the form is at least three inches by three inches. Otherwise, it won't cut very well. You should use regular paper for this.

Now, to make this work, you need to put the paper onto the cutting mat. You should have one of those, so take it right now and remove the attached film. Put a corner of the form to the area where you are directed to align the paper corners. From there, push the form directly onto the cutting mat for proper adherence. Once you do that, you just load it into the machine, following the arrows. You'll want to keep the paper firmly on the mat.

Press the "load paper" key that you see as you do this. If it doesn't take for some reason, press the unload paper key, and try this again until it shows up.

Now, BEFORE YOU DO ANY CUTTING FOR YOUR DESIGN, YOU SHOULD always have a test cut in place. Some people don't do this, but it's incredibly helpful when learning how to use a Cricut. Otherwise, you won't get the pressure correct in some cases, so get in the habit of doing it for your pieces.

For effective cutting, it is recommended that the paper to be cut should not be lesser than 3″ × 3″. Cardstock is also recommended in order to achieve the best result. In case you are using the machine for the first time, you can become familiar with the device by practicing with cheaper materials.

In order to cut a paper on the machine, the form should be placed on the cutting mat. It is better to first try it with a form of 6" × 12" if you are not used to the machine. First, remove the protective film of the cutting mat.

You will then ensure that a corner of the paper is aligned. Proceed by pressing the writing unto the cutting mat to make it fit in well.

Once this is done, the paper is ready to be cut. In case you want to choose other paper sizes, check the Advanced Operations.

How to Remove Your Cuts from Cutting Mat

The machine will automatically load the mat and the paper after pressing the load paper key. In the rare occurrence that this does not happen, don't hesitate to push the Unload Paper key.

Once you press the Unload Paper key, you will go through the procedure again. It should work unless there is an issue with the machine. A likely problem is the unavailability of up to 1 ft. (30.5 cm) of clear space.

This clear space is needed in the front and back of the Cricut machine for paper movement.

Removing your cut from the mat is easy, but complicated. Personally, I ran into the issue of it being more involved with vinyl projects since they love to just stick around there. But we'll explain how you can create significant cuts and remove them, as well.

THE FIRST THING TO REMEMBER IS TO MAKE SURE THAT YOU'RE USING the right mat. The light grip ones are good for very soft material, with the pink one being one of the strongest, and only to be used with the Cricut Maker. Once the design is cut, you'll probably be eager about removing the project directly from the mat, but one of the problems with this is that often, the project will be ruined if you're not careful. Instead of pulling the project from the mat itself, bend the mat within your hand, and push it away from the project, since this will loosen it from the carpet. Bend this both horizontally and vertically, so that the adhesive releases the project.

Use this spatula to lightly pull on the vinyl, until you can grab it from the corner and lift it up. Otherwise, you risk curling it or tearing the mat, which is what we don't want.

You will notice that Cricut mats are incredibly sticky, and if you don't have a Cricut spatula on hand or don't want to spend the money, metal spatulas will work, too. You can put the paper on a flat surface and then lightly remove it. But always be careful when removing these items.

HOW TO DESIGN WITH CRICUT MAKER

When you see the finished product from a Cricut machine, you will definitely be blown away. The neatness and appealing look of a typical project done with the Cricut machine will take your breath away. However, only a few people understand the process involved in the creation of such unique designs.

Curious to know how the Cricut machine is able to cut out materials effectively? You are reading the right book. There are three significant steps involved when using the Cricut machine:

HAVE A DESIGN

If you have a PC, you can access the Cricut Design Space to access the library of designs. If you have a Mac, you can access the same platform to select a vast variety of formats. In case you don't have any of these two but possesses an iPhone or iPad, you can use the Design Space for iOS.

If what you have is an android, you are covered as well. This is because you can take advantage of the Design Space for Android. These are online platforms where you can select any design that best suits your taste.

You can also customize a ready-made design to suit your need. For example, you can resize it or modify the shape. You can also add a text or image as you wish till you have the design just as you want it.

PREPARE THE MACHINE

Having selected the design, you intend cutting out with the machine, you are ready for the next step. The device needs to be prepared by turning it on. Once you switch on the device, you actually don't need to do anything.

You don't have to press any button unless you are using the machine for the first time. In that case, the device will give you instructions on what to do. It is that simple.

That is why both beginners and experts can make use of the Cricut machine without issues. Your computer or phone will have to be paired with the device via Bluetooth for the first time. However, this will not be needed subsequently because the machine will remember the pairing.

Hence, once the machine is switched on, the pairing between the phone and the machine becomes automatic. The implication of this is that once the machine is switched on, the machine is ready. The next step is to send the design to the machine.

SEND THE DESIGN TO THE MACHINE

This is the last stage of the process of cutting with the Cricut machine. Once the machine is powered on, at the top right corner of the screen, you will see the Make It button. This button is a big green button on the Cricut Design Space.

The first thing the software does is to preview the various mats you have. A mat represents a sheet of material; hence, having two different colors in your project implies two rugs. There are times that your project can be a combination of a fabric and a paper.

The machine will request that you pick the particular material you want to use for the first mat. Simply choose whether it is paper, vinyl, fabric, leather, or any other material. Once you do this, the machine will automatically adjust pressure, speed, and the brush blade as necessary.

Hence, just ensure you do your part of instructing the machine to do your bidding as desired. You can trust the Cricut machine from that point to do all that is needed for a perfect project. After the machine has adjusted itself to cut, you will put the material into the Cricut cutting mat.

It is obvious that you don't have to be a genius before you are qualified to use the machine. The instructions are simplified such that anyone who can understand basic English language can use it. Therefore, if you have been thinking that you might not be able to operate this machine, you are wrong.

How to Clean The Cricut Maker

With an extended period of use, it is likely that your machine would have collected dirt and grime. So, here are some tips on how you can clean your machine and keep it looking and working as new.

Prior to cleaning the machine, make sure that it has been powered off and disconnected from the power source.

Use a microfiber cloth or a piece of soft clean cloth sprayed with a glass cleaning solution to clean the machine.

In the case of static electricity build-up on the machine due to dust or paper particles, use the same cloth to wipe off the residues and get rid of the static from the machine.

For grease build up on the bar that allows the carriage travels, use a soft cloth or tissue or cotton swab and gently remove the oil from the machine.

Do not use nail polish remover or any other acetone-containing solution to clean the machine, as it may permanently damage the plastic shell of the machine.

To keep the machine running smoothly, you may want to grease it following the instructions below:

Power off your machine and carefully push the "Cut Smart" carriage to the left of the machine.

Use a tissue to wipe the carriage bar (located in front of the belt).

Now, carefully move the bar to the right and clean again with the tissue.

Carefully move the bar to the center and use a cotton swab to lubricate both sides of the carriage by applying a light coating of grease around the bar to form a 1/4-inch ring on each side of the carriage.

In order to evenly distribute the grease on the carriage, slowly move the carriage from one end to another a couple of times and wipe off any excessive oil.

Note – It is recommended to use grease packet supplied by Cricut only, and no other grease from a third party should be used.

CRICUT DESIGN SPACE SOFTWARE FOR CRICUT MAKER

For craft enthusiasts and people that love the Cricut die cutting system, it is no longer news that digital die cutting units are incredibly restrictive.

They mostly allow users to cut a small number of fonts and they are not cheap at all.

Thankfully, there are a few programs out there that have managed to open Cricut to enable them to cut designs, True Type fonts created by users and many more.

Below is a list of the best third-party software to use with Cricut.

MAKE THE CUT

This is an excellent third- party Cricut Design software that comes with simple but highly effective design features e.g. it packs quick lattice tools, and it can convert raster images into vectors for cutting. The program has been around for some time. Some of the most outstanding features of the tool include;

It comes with advanced editing tools, and it is quite easy to use (even for a newbie) because the user interface is effortless to learn.

The software works with many file formats and it also uses TrueType fonts

The software comes with Pixel trace tool that allows users to take and convert raster graphics into vector paths for cutting.

Make The Cut is a user-friendly and flexible Cricut related software that adds more utility to the digital die cutting machine that is usually limited in terms of usage and application.

SURE CUTS A LOT

The Sure Cuts A Lot software gives users complete control of their designs without the restrictions of cartridges featured in Cricut DesignStudio.

Users must install a firmware update to their Cricut die cutting machine; however, they can do this for free by downloading the trial version of DesignStudio. It is a straightforward task to perform.

Some of the features of the Sure Cuts A lot software include;

It allows users to use the OpenType and TrueType fonts.

It is the one and only Cricut Design tool available that comes with freestyle drawing tools.

It allows users t\o create unique designs with basic drawing and editing tools.

The program works with Silhouette, Craft ROBO, and Wishblade die cutting machines.

It is specifically designed to open up all of Cricut's cutting features and abilities.

It allows users to edit the individual nodes the make up the path.

It comes with an auto trace feature that converts raster graphics into vector images

CRICUT DESIGNSTUDIO

Cricut DesignStudio, a product of ProvoCraft is a program that allows users to connect Cricut to a personal computer so that they can do much more with Cricut fonts and shapes.

For those that don't know, Provo Craft is the same company that manufactures Cricut die cutting machines. With the aid of various tools, this Cricut software allows users to adjust fonts and shapes.

Some of the best features of the software include;

Users have the option of previewing and creating designs with different images from the Cricut library.

Users will have to purchase a cartridge to cut.

The software comes with a high level of customization to the Cricut library, and the extra features are beneficial

People that use this software are still limited to the same shapes and fonts from the cartridges they own, but bearing in mind the tools that are packed in the program, that is not an issue.

The program remains a perfect option to use alongside your Cricut, and you'll be able to get the best out of its features. To know more about the software, go to their official website.

MAKING YOUR FIRST PROJECT IDEA

Now that you have everything set to go, it's time to start with your first project. If this is the first time that you are using a Cricut Machine, then do follow the guidelines we will be presenting in this chapter as they will help you avoid some of the most common mistakes.

On the whole, using a Cricut Machine and the Design Space software is pretty straightforward. This means that you don't need any specialized knowledge to make fair use of this software. Of course, if you have used design software in the past, then that experience will certainly come in handy. Nevertheless, you don't need to have any previous experience to make your creations come to life.

So, here are five useful tips that you can put into practice when starting with your very first projects.

DO YOUR HOMEWORK

When starting out, it's always a good idea to go over sample project ideas before you actually start cutting. In this book, you will find great project ideas which you can put into practice right away. Do, it's a great idea to go over these ideas before you begin designing your creations. In addition, the internet is filled with great design ideas. So, you can poach some of these ideas and use them for your benefit. On the whole, there are really talented and creative designers out there who have come up with sample projects to help new users get the hang of the Cricut Machine.

As you gain more practice and proficiency with the Cricut Machine, it's a good idea to keep perusing project ideas. It could be that you find images which you can later customize to your own liking. This will make it easier for you to get the hang of the types of projects you can come up with. Over time, you will be able to make your ideas from scratch!

START SMALL

When you don't have much experience with the Cricut Machine and Design Space, it's a good idea to start with small projects. Such projects don't take up a lot of time and are easy to put together. As you gain more experience and proficiency, you can tackle bigger and bigger projects. But when starting out, it's always a good idea to tackle smaller projects. That way, you won't become overwhelmed by the complexity of a larger project.

Also, it's essential to consider that if things don't go quite as planned, you won't feel frustrated by this. So, you will be able to manage your skills and expectations in such a way that you won't get discouraged early on.

PRACTICE MAKES PERFECT

Like anything in life, becoming a pro with the Cricut Machine and Design Space take time and practice. Now, this doesn't mean that you need weeks and weeks of training and study. What it does mean is that the more projects you take on, the easier it will become to use the Cricut Machine and Design Space. So, it definitely helps to take on more and more projects.

Of course, we all have pretty tight schedules nowadays. So, it's not precisely simple to sit down at your computer and work for hours on end on projects. Yet, if you can dedicate a couple of hours a week to your projects, you will find that it will really help you get the most out of the Cricut Machine. In this manner, you will quickly build up your proficiency. Before you know it, you will be coming up with genuinely creative and innovative ideas.

EASY DOES IT

One of the first reactions that newbies to the Cricut Machine get is to be gung-ho about using their brand-new machine. However, enthusiasm tends to wear off. This is why it's a good idea to take on one project at a time. You see, when you get ahead of yourself and take on multiple projects at once, things can get a bit muddled. While there is nothing wrong with being aggressive and trying to make the most out of your new machine, taking on multiple projects early on can be a bit confusing and potentially overwhelming. This might even lead you to feel discouraged. So, the perfect antidote to this point is to take on one project at a time. The sense of satisfaction that you get from completing your very first projects is indescribable.

DRAW OUT YOUR IDEA ON PAPER FIRST

Design Space is a fantastic tool. It is the perfect companion that enables you to translate the ideas in your head to practical applications. As such, you can put its instruments to fair use without much complication and with relative ease.

However, one of the most significant setbacks that first-time users run into is not having a clear picture in their minds about what they would like to do. This can lead you to feel dissatisfied with your creations. Also, it can make finalizing a design a bit challenging.

This is why we recommend that you sketch out your idea on a piece of paper first. This will help you to organize your thoughts before hitting Design Space. While the finished product may differ significantly, it certainly helps to have a good idea of what you plan to do. This technique is similar to what writers do with a storyboard. They outline the story before writing. That way, they know where they will begin and where they will end. If they change their mind along the way, that's fine. The main point is to avoid having your ideas go down paths that won't lead anywhere practical.

How to Upload Images with a Cricut Maker

There are many images to choose from in the library, but it also encourages the use of your images. Images are categorized into two types. The first type is Image, and the second is the Pattern.

IMAGES:

Images also have two types, Basic and the other one is Vector.

Necessary images like JPG, GIF, PNG, are uploaded as one layer. Uploading the image will require a few steps that the software will guide through. There are two ways to use the picture.

First, by print and cut features, print the image and then calibrate the Cricut to cut around it.

Second, is to cut only the outer edges of the image directly on the machine.

Vector files come in SVG Dxf files, which are not uploaded as a single layer but multiple layers. Other imported images from different software can also be uploaded. You can search the uploaded image by searching its name/tag. Also, all uploaded images can be seen by applying the filter uploaded.

PATTERN:

Uploaded patterns can be seen in the Layers Attributes Panel under the Pattern option. Files that can be uploaded are .jpg .png .gif .bmp. When uploading, choose appropriate tags and name for easy searching. You can also access this by clicking uploaded in Patterns filter.

HOW TO UPLOAD AN IMAGE FROM PHOTOSHOP?

Cricut Design Space does not allow you to make changes to the images that you want to use. If changes are to be made to the design, then another software like Adobe Photoshop should be used first. Adobe Photoshop does not save vector files, so if the picture has multiple layers, it will be compressed into one. Images best work in jpg. Files, but others can also be used.

MIKE DAWSON

Firstly make the required changes in the image using Photoshop. Then save the file in jpg. Format and name it.

How to select an image?

It is effortless to select an image onto the Canvas. There are four methods for this task:

First, select an image from inside the Canvas. When an image is selected, it will be shown in the Layers Panel in the highlighted form, and a bounding box will appear around the image.

Or, select an image from the Layers Panel. This will also like the print on your Canvas

Another option is to select an image from drawing a box. Then draw a box around the idea that it is entirely inside it. The package will turn blue, and the image will be selected.

If there is one image, select the 'Select All' option. If there is more than one image, then all of them will be chosen.

Working with uploaded photos

Select the option for upload images under the upload page

If it is a photo, then select the option 'Complex Image' under the upload screen. Then click 'Continue.'

For the photo to retain its details, it should be used in print and cut. It is done by default, and it is saved as print and cut image. Now click save.

Back on your upload screen, click on the photo and then click insert. The image is now ready to use.

This photo can be manipulated using different tools such as slip tool, or flatten tool. The slip tool can be used to cut the picture or cut images out of the photo. The flatten tool can insert different pictures on the photo.

PATTERNS

Select the option for upload pattern under the upload screen.

Browse the photo using its name and selected.

Name and add appropriate tags to your photo to make searching easy.

A shape can be used to cut the image to make a pattern. First, insert a form in the Canvas. Open the 'Layers Attributes Panel' under the 'Image Layers' option. Now select 'Line Types' and then 'Patterns.' Different patterns will open along with the photo. Select the desired photo and fill the shape.

Use different editing tools to your likings, like rotate, scale, pan, and mirror.

CUT VINYL WITH A CRICUT MAKER

First, place the Vinyl liner side down onto the Standard grip mat. Then put it inside the machine after selecting the design. Push the go button to start.

For a smooth placement of the vinyl, you should use vinyl transfer tape. Transfer tape is a kind of pre-mask that transfer vinyl graphics to a substrate after being cut and weeded.

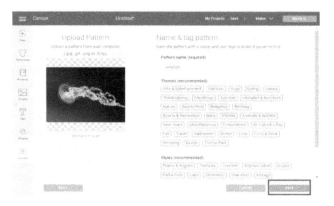

AFTER CUTTING IS DONE, REMOVE THE NEGATIVES OF THE IMAGE BY a weeder or a tweezer, only leaving the wanted design on the mat. Now remove the Transfer Tape liner. Carefully with the sticky side down, place it on the mat with the system. Gently press to remove any air bubbles.

Whatever surface you want the design on, it should be clean and dry. Carefully place the vinyl on the body and gently press it down. Remove the tap by peeling it off at a 45-degree angle. If it is difficult, burnish it by using a scrapper.

HOW TO MAKE STICKERS

There are a lot of designs and decors one can use the Cricut machine to create. Some of the stickers one can use the machine to create and cut are as follows:

- Cupcake stickers

- Sticky labels
- Planner stickers
- Safari animal sticker
- Vinyl sticker for car windows amid any other types of sticker your heart so desires

Now let us explore individual designs that can be effected with the machine.

PROCEDURE FOR MAKING CUPCAKE STICKERS

The supplies needed for this brand of stickers are:

- the Cricut machine,
- printable sticker paper,
- an inkjet printer.

The following are the steps to follow in creating cupcake stickers:

- Log in to the Cricut design spaces.
- Start a new project and click on the Images icon on the left side of the screen.
- Select the cupcake image(s) you want.
- Highlight the whole image and use the Flatten button to solidify the image as one whole piece.
- Resize the image to the appropriate size you need. You realize this by clicking on the image then dragging the right side of the box to the size you desire.
- Click Save at the top left to save your project. Save it to be a Print and Cut image, after which you click the Make It button at the right hand of the screen.
- Examine the end result and click Continue if it's what you expected. This will lead you to print the design onto the paper.
- Adjust the dial on the Cricut machine to the required settings.
- Place the sticker paper on the cutting mat.

- Load the cutting mat into the machine, and push it against the rollers.
- Press the Load/Unload button and then the Go button to cut the stickers.
- Sit back and relax while you watch the Cricut machine cut your designed stickers for you.

PROCEDURES FOR MAKING STICKY LABELS

Supplies needed are as follows:

- Cricut machine
- Printable sticker paper
- Inkjet printer

Take the next few steps to bring this sticker to life:

- Log in to the Cricut design space.
- Start a new project.
- Click on the Text icon and input your text.
- Select the font of your desire from the available font package.
- Highlight the texts and change the color by using the available colors on the color tray.
- Click on the Print option to change the file to a print file from a cut file.
- Click on the Ungroup icon to adjust the spacing of the text.

After adjusting the spaces, highlight all and use the Group icon to make them one whole piece again.

- Click on the Shape icon and insert a shape.
- If it's a rectangle you need, insert a square, unlock the shape, and drag it to a rectangle.
- Change the shape's color using the color tray.
- Highlight the text and use the Align drop-down box.

- Make use of the Move to Front icon to move the text to front.
- Highlight the design and click on Group.
- Duplicate the label as much as you want.
- Highlight the whole design and use the Flatten icon to keep it together during printing.
- Highlight the design and right-click then select Attach.
- Click on the Go button and print the design on the printable sticker paper.
- Adjust the dial on the Cricut machine to the required settings.
- Place the sticker paper on the cutting mat.
- Load the cutting mat into the machine, and push it against the rollers.
- Press the Load/Unload button and then the Go button to cut the stickers.

Your sticky label is ready for use.

WORKING WITH IMAGES/EDIT PANEL

The blank Edit Bar is shown in the picture below. All the functions that can be seen on the Edit Bar are explained right after, so we can get you started on creating your first craft project on Design Space.

UNDO/REDO – YOU CAN USE THE "UNDO" BUTTON TO REVERT TO your previous state and use the "Redo" button to perform the step that was undone.

Linetype – All the way, the machine can interact with the design base material on the mat, namely, Cut, Draw, Score, Engrave, Deboss, Perf, and Wavy are called as "Linetype."

Linetype Swatch – If you would like to choose additional layer attributes for your design, you can select the "Linetype swatch." The alternatives available will be updated on the basis of the "Linetype" you selected. When the "Cut" option is chosen, you will notice a solid line next to the "Linetype" icon, an outline if the "Draw" is determined, and when the "Score" is chosen, a "/" will be visible. Here are some details on the features that will be available for your selected "Linetype."

CUT ATTRIBUTES

Material colors – You can select the desired color on the "Material colors palette" to instantly match the colors of your project. A checkmark will be displayed in the "color swatch" for the design layer that you are working on.

Primary colors – You will also be able to select a color from the "basic color palette."

Advanced – You can move the slider to choose a color from the "custom color picker," or if you know precisely the "hex" numbers for your desired color, simply plug those numbers in, and you will get that color for your design.

Draw Attributes – If you have selected the "Draw" Linetype, you will be given the option to "Choose a Cricut pen type" from the dropdown. The colors available for your selected "pen type" will be displayed in the list accordingly.

Print - You can select this option for accessing "Print Then Cut" color and pattern choices.

Fill Swatch – If you would like to choose from other Fill attributes for a layer, click on the

Original Artwork – If you are not excited about the fill of the design and want to restore to the original image, you can do this by selecting "Original artwork."

Color - You can choose your desired color from the current material colors, a primary colors palette, the custom color picker, or by entering a hex color code.

Pattern - You could also fill an image or text layer with a design. If you filter the pattern selection by color, it will be easier to find the right way, which you can further modify using the "Edit Pattern" tools.

Size – If you need to alter the height or width of an object, then you can simply type in the exact dimensions in the given boxes or click on the "stepper" to increase or decreases the size while looking at the changes on your design. Remember to first lock the image aspect ratio by clicking on the "Lock" icon to ensure that, as you modify one dimension, the whole image will be changed in the same proportion.

Rotate – You will be able to modify the angle of the selected item using the stepper, or you can type in the exact degree by which you want to alter the image.

More – If your screen resolution doesn't allow the complete Edit Bar to be visible, then you would see a "More" drop-down containing the features that do not appear on your screen.

Position – You can use this option to change the status of your selected item using the stepper, or you can type in the exact distance by which you want to move the image from the top-left corner of the Canvas.

EDITING FONTS

If you decided to add text to your design or select a "text object" on the Canvas or select a "text layer" in the Layers Panel, the "Text Edit Bar" will be displayed directly below the image "Edit Bar" on your screen. All the functions that can be seen on the "Text Edit Bar" are shown in the picture and explained below.

FONT – THIS WILL PROVIDE YOU A LIST OF CRICUT FONTS ALONG with all the fonts available on your computer.

Font Drop-Down – You will be able to view all the fonts available to you or may choose to view just the Cricut fonts, or only fonts installed on your system, or all the fonts at the same time, using the "Font Drop-Down." Font filters may also be searched and applied. Just browse the font list and choose your desired font to be applied to the selected text.

Font Filter – You can use this feature for filtering the fonts by category and alter the fonts that are displayed in the "Font Type" menu.

All Fonts – To view all available fonts that can be used for your project.

System Fonts – To view only the fonts installed on your system.

Cricut Fonts – To view just the fonts from the Cricut library.

Single Layer Fonts – To view fonts containing only a single layer.

Writing Style Fonts - To view fonts that are designed particularly to be written by hand. These fonts are characterized by letters with a single stroke that makes them appear like handwritten letters.

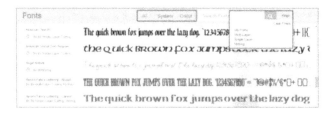

STYLE – THIS FEATURE WILL ALLOW YOU TO SELECT THE TYPE OF

your font, such as regular, bold, italic, and bold italic. You may also see the option of "writing" when the appropriate font has been selected. Remember, the style of Cricut fonts may differ from your system fonts.

Font Size – You can adjust the size of the fonts by typing in the desired point size or using the stepper to change the font size by 1 point gradually.

CRICUT SCRAPBOOKING

Scrapbooking can verge on a fixation for us. We're continually attempting to make that ideal page design or locate that perfect little touch that will make our scrapbooks that significantly improved. You can utilize the Cricut machine to make kick the bucket cuts of scrapbook page formats and afterward rapidly offer them to other fans such as yourself. On the off chance that it is your obsession, at that point it will be no issue thinking of some amazing plans!

SOLVING THE MOST COMMON PROBLEM WHEN USING CRICUT Maker

FIXING CRICUT DESIGN SPACE ISSUES

When you put everything into consideration, it is safe to say that the Design Space software is excellent.

No system is perfect, and there's always room for improvements, but on the whole, the software works excellently for several projects. However, there are a couple of related issues that are predominant with the software, including; freezing, slow loading, crashing and not opening at all. When you're faced with these issues, there are several things you can do to fix them, including;

. . .

SLOW INTERNET CONNECTION

You must understand that a slow internet connection is one of the leading causes of Design Space problems without saying much. Poor internet connection translates into problems for the software because it requires consistent download and upload speeds to function optimally.

Several websites only require good download speeds e.g. YouTube, thus users on these sites can do away with slow upload speeds. However, unlike those sites, Cricut Design Space requires good upload and download speeds to function optimally because users are always sending and receiving information as they progress with their designs.

Note: If you're using a modem, you're likely to have a more stable connection if you move closer to it.

RUN A SPEED TEST

You can use a service like Ookla to run an internet speed test.

For Design Space to run optimally, Cricut specifies the following;

- Broadband connection
- Minimum 1 – 2 Mbps Upload
- Minimum 2 – 3 Mbps Download

After running the speed test, if the results are not good, and you are convinced that the connection is affecting to your Design space issues, you should wait until the connection improves or you call your service providers. There is also the option of switching to a new internet service provider with a proper internet connection.

BACKGROUND PROGRAMS

If you're running too many background programs while using Design Space, it might also be a problem.

Some multi-tasking crafters are fond of engaging in different activities while designing on Design Space. For example, some simultaneously chat on Facebook, while downloading movies, watching videos on YouTube, and designing on Design Space. These activities will affect your app and make it malfunction badly, thus it is important to shut down other projects and focus solely on Design Space.

While it is important to close other apps and shut down other activities, there are other things should also do;

- Run a malware check
- If you're using windows, you should upgrade you drivers
- Clear your history and cache
- Defragment your hard drive
- Check your anti-virus software and update if needed

If you execute these tests, it might speed up the system, or even solve all related problems.

Your Browser

Your Design Space software might be having issues due to your system browser.

For you to access Design Space, Cricut recommends using the latest version of the browser you use. Be it Edge, Chrome, Firefox or Mozilla; just make sure that it is up to date. If it refuses to work on a particular browser, open it in another browser to see if it works. Although the reasons are unknown, sometimes its works and even works perfectly.

Contact Cricut

If you've tried all possible options and nothing works, you may have to call Cricut customer care to look into the issues you're faced with.

Cricut Joy

Machine Setup and How to Prepare the Material

One way or another, you found yourself in possession of a Cricut joy machine and you have been worried about setting it up correctly? Well, there are lots of people like you on this table. Setting up your machine could look somehow complicated or tedious. However, this section is majorly written to guide you through it; the unboxing process and the setting up. So, relax and bring that Cricut machine out wherever you've stashed it. It takes approximately 1 hour to finish setting up a Cricut machine. With this guide, you should be done in less than an hour. Let's get right on it, shall we?

OPENING THE BOX

To make sure that we are together all the way through, we will go through even the most trivial step; opening the box.

You should be having a number of boxes right now in front of you if you went for the whole Cricut bundle. And there should be a big box among those boxes which contains the Cricut joy machine itself. If you open that big box, the first thing you should find is a Welcome packet, most of the tools will be in that packet. You should find a welcome book, rotary blade and cover, a USB cable, a fine-point pen, a packet that contains your first die-cutting project. The USB cable is sometimes the last thing you'll see in this packet, it's hidden under every other stuff. Underneath this welcome packet is your Cricut joy machine.

UNWRAPPING YOUR CRICUT JOY MACHINE AND SUPPLIES

We are getting to the exciting part. Let's unwrap your machine and find out what's inside.

When trying to unwrap your machine, you'll find it covered in a protective wrapper that looks filmy and also with a cellophane layer. Try to carefully unwrap the top foam layer so you can see the machine. After that, remove the remaining part of the Styrofoam that protects the inner machine housing.

When you unbox the whole casing, you should expect to find the following tools;

- Cricut Machine
- USB and Power Cables
- Rotatory blade with housing.
- Fine point blade with housing
- Fine point pen.
- Light-Grip and Fabric-Grip Mats (12 x 12)

SETTING UP YOUR CRICUT JOY MACHINE

Once they are all connected, open your computer browser to continue the setup. Visit the Cricut Sign-in Page and click on the "Sign in" icon. You will have to either sign in with your account details or create a new account for yourself if you don't already have one. This is necessary so as to be able to access the Cricut Design Space.

If you do not have an active account yet, don't bother to fill any information on the sign-in fields. Click on the "Create Cricut ID" in the green box and then fill out every field with the required information and click on "Submit."

NOW, IT'S TIME TO LINK YOUR MACHINE TO YOUR ACCOUNT. IT takes some people a lot of time to finish this part successfully. To make it easier, follow the procedures below.

After signing in, go to the upper left corner of the page and click on the drop-down menu icon (with three lines) beside "Home."\

When the drop-down menu appears, select the "New Machine Setup."

On the next screen that pops up, click on your Cricut machine model.

ANOTHER WEBPAGE WILL APPEAR WITH INSTRUCTIONS ON HOW TO CONNECT YOUR MACHINE. Follow the instruction accordingly.

When you follow the instructions, it automatically detects your machine and prompts you to download and install the software.

The site is user-friendly, so you'll be directed on how to go about the installation. And if you already have an account, you may still need to download it again. Cricut updates their design space often, there could be some new tools in the latest version that you don't have access to. It only takes about five minutes to get the installation done.

CARTRIDGE

Designs are produced using parts put away on cartridges. Every cartridge accompanies a console overlay and guidance booklet. The plastic console overlay demonstrates key determinations for that cartridge as it were. Anyway, as of late Provo Craft has discharged an "All-inclusive Overlay" perfect with all cartridges discharged after August 1, 2013. The motivation behind the all-inclusive overlay is to simplify the way toward slicing by just learning one console overlay instead of learning the overlay for every individual cartridge. Designs can be removed on a PC with the Cricut Design Studio programming, on a USB associated Gypsy machine, or can be legitimately inputted on the Cricut machine utilizing the console overlay. There are two kinds of cartridges shape and textual style. Every cartridge has an assortment of imaginative highlights that can consider several different cuts from only one cartridge.

More than 275 cartridges are accessible (independently from the machine), containing textual styles and shapes, with new ones included monthly. While a few cartridges are conventional in substance, Cricut has to permit Disney, Pixar, Nickelodeon, Sesame Street, DC Comics and Hello Kitty. The Cricut line has a scope of costs. The cartridges are compatible, even though not all alternatives on a cartridge might be accessible with the little machines. All cartridges work just with Cricut programming. They must be enrolled to a solitary client for use and can't be sold or given away. A cartridge obtained for a suspended machine will probably wind up futile at the point the machine is ended. Cricut maintains whatever authority is needed to suspend support for certain product renditions whenever, which can make a few cartridges quickly out of date.

The Cricut joy Craft Room programming empowers clients to join pictures from different cartridges, consolidate pictures, and stretch/turn pictures; it doesn't take into account the formation of discretionary designs. It additionally empowers the client to see the pictures showed on-screen before starting the cutting procedure so that the final product can be seen in advance.

LOADING YOUR PAPER

To load paper into a Cricut machine, you'll want to make sure that the paper is at least three inches by three inches. Otherwise, it won't cut very well. You should use regular paper for this.

Now, to make this work, you need to put the paper onto the cutting mat. You should have one of those, so take it right now and remove the attached film. Put a corner of the paper to the area where you are directed to align the paper corners. From there, push the paper directly onto the cutting mat for proper adherence. Once you do that, you just load it into the machine, following the arrows. You'll want to keep the paper firmly on the mat.

Press the "load paper" key that you see as you do this. If it doesn't take for some reason, press the unload paper key, and try this again until it shows up.

Before you do any cutting for your design, you should always have a test cut in place. Some people don't do this, but it's incredibly helpful when learning how to use a Cricut. Otherwise, you won't get the pressure correct in some cases, so get in the habit of doing it for your pieces.

SELECTING SHAPES, LETTERS, AND PHRASES

When you're creating your Design Space design, you usually begin by using letters, shapes, numbers, or different fonts. These are the basics, and they're incredibly easy.

To make text, you just press the text tool on the left-hand side and type out your text. For example, write the word hello, or joy, or whatever you want to use.

You can choose different Cricut or system fonts, too. Cricut ones will be in green, and if you have Cricut Access, this is a great way to begin using this. You can sort these, too, so you don't end up accidentally paying for a font.

The Cricut ones are supposed to be made for Cricut, so you know they'll look good. Design Space also lets you put them closer together so they can be cut with a singular cut. You can change this by going to line spacing and adjusting as needed.

Adding shapes is pretty easy, as well. In Design Space, choose the shapes option. Once you click it, the window will then pop out, and you'll have a wonderful array of different shapes that you can use with just one click. Choose your shape, and from there, put it in the space. Drag the corners in order to make this bigger or smaller.

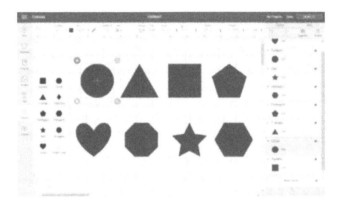

THERE IS ALSO THE SCORE LINE, WHICH CREATES A FOLDING LINE FOR you to use. Personally, if you're thinking of trying to make a card at first, I suggest using this.

Once you've chosen the design, it's time for you to start cutting.

HOW TO REMOVE YOUR CUTS FROM CUTTING MAT

For placing your material to cut it on the mat, it's essential to know the placement. First, the mat's cover should be removed and placed elsewhere. The Cricut maker comes with a blue Light Grip mat, which is used for cutting paper mainly. The match will be slightly sticky for the suitable placement of the material. When loading, the material should be placed in the top left corner of the mat. Be sure to press down gently so that the material could be evened out. Place the top of the mat in the guides of the machine. Gently press on the rollers and press the load/to unload the button on top of the Cricut. Once loaded up, the software will tell you the next step. After the project has been finished, the material needs to be unloaded. Press on the load/unload button and take out the mat from the machine. The right way to remove the material from the mat is to be placed on a level surface, and the mat should be peeled off. A scrapper or a tweezer can peel off the remaining scraps.

How to design With Cricut Joy

When you break it down to its most basic operation, the Cricut joy does two things. It cuts, and it draws. However, these two functions have over a million uses and can be used on hundreds of materials, making it a truly versatile crafting powerhouse. Breaking it down to these two features seems almost like an injustice to the adaptability and versatility that this machine truly has.

There are more than 50 crafts you can do using your Cricut joy machine. Here, I will discuss in simple terms these amazing items:

Cut fabrics: the rotary blade was designed to cut seamlessly through any fabric including silk, denim, chiffon, and heavy canvass. Coupled with the mat, hundreds of fabrics can be cut without any backing. This is amazing!

Vinyl Decals and stickers: Is cutting vinyl decals and stickers your hobby, then you need Cricut Maker machine as your companion. Get the design inputted in the Design Space Software and instruct the machine to cut. As easy as that. The delivery will be wonderful. So what are you waiting for? Get to work!

Greeting Cards: The power and precision of the Cricut Maker makes cutting of paper and makes greeting cards craft less tedious and saves ample time. Your Christmas cards, birthday cards, success cards and other greeting cards will be delivered with accurate, unique and amazing style.

How to Clean The Cricut Joy

If you want your Cricut machine to last for a long time, you must keep a routine basis. This means appropriately cleaning and maintaining cutting mats and blades.

Cricut machine maintenance

When the Cricut machine is used, eventually, paper particles will inevitably lead to reverse charging, dust, and debris. Also, the fat in the device will begin to stick to the track carriage.

If you want your machine to last long, then you should be cleaned regularly, or otherwise, be damaged prematurely. Here are some cleaning tips to help clean out the engine.

Before cleaning the device, disconnect it from the electrical outlet. This will prevent electrocution or any other accidents that may damage the device or damage.

Apply a small layer of fat on both sides of the carriage smart cut around the bar so that they form a ring is a quarter inch on both sides.

To make fat even become the car, push the smart carriage cut on both sides slowly and repeatedly.

Clean any grease that stained the bar while I was oiling the machine.

You can buy a pack of pasta Cricut. This works better than using a third-party package paste for the machine.

It will not get damaged. This is especially true if the Cricut machine makes a squeaking sound after using another product grease.

This process is almost the same as lubricating the machine maker Cricut too.

MAINTAINING THE CRICUT CUTTING MAT

You also have to clean and maintain your Cricut cutting mat because cutting is carried out.

If the cutting is not clean, it can stain the machine. Also, if your cutting mat has left grip, you can spoil your designs and creations.

When your carpet is no longer sticky because of debris and dirt, cleaning and making it sticky again bring back life.

I will mention the solutions that are not ideal for rose-cut mats, just for green, blue, and purple.

THERE ARE MANY WAYS TO CLEAN YOUR CUTTING MAT.

THE USE OF WET WIPES FOR BABIES:

Make use of baby unscented bleach-free wipes without alcohol to clean your carpet. Must use wipes lighter babies can be found so that no lotions, corn starch, solvent or oil is added to the cutting base. If not, you could affect the adhesion and adhesive carpet. Also, after cleaning, let it dry completely before using it.

Using a sticky lint roller

You can also use a roll of tape if not find a sticky lint roller. Run the roll through the mat to get rid of hair, fibers, dust particles, and paper particles.

. . .

Using hot soapy water

You can also clean the carpet with soap and warm water. You must use the flattest possible soap also to not mess with the mat. Use a clean

Cloth, sponge, soft brush, or Magic Eraser. Also, rinse thoroughly and do not use until completely dry.

The use of an adhesive remover

For heavy-duty cleaning, you must use a reliable adhesive remover to clean appropriately. A to use an adhesive remover, read the instructions properly before you start.

Then spray a small amount on the mat and spread with a scraper or anything that can act as a scraper record.

How to make your sticky mat Cut Again

After washing or cleaning, the cutting mat must again make them sticky.

The most advisable way to do their sticky mat is again by adding glue to it. Obtain a solid stick glue-like Zig Pen 2-Way and apply it on the inside of the rug. Then, cerebrovascular accident glues around the mat and make sure there is no residue of glue on the edges of the carpet.

After about 30 minutes, the glue will become clear. If the cutting mat turns out to be too sticky after applying the glue, you can be used a piece of fabric to reduce the adhesive pressing the material into parts of the mat that are very sticky.

You can also use sticky adhesives or spray adhesives that are ideal for cutting mats.

General maintenance

When the carpet is not in use, it is covered with a transparent cover film so that the dust and hair are not accumulated on the surface of the rug.

Carefully manage their mats. If you want to make sure that the adhesive is not damaged, do not touch the sticky surface with your hands.

Always make sure that your carpet to dry completely before using or concealment. Do not use heat when the mat to dry but can be placed in front of a fan. Also, make sure that is drying hang both sides will dry up.

MAINTAINING THE CRICUT CUTTING BLADE

You can use your Cricut beautiful tip sheet over a year if maintained properly! The same goes for other types of cutting blades. When securing the Cricut cutting blade, you have to keep it sharp all the time, so they do not wear out.

Keep your sharp blade essential because it can damage your materials and waste caused if it is not. Also, if you do not keep your knives, you will have to replace them frequently.

KEEPING YOUR BLADE SHARP CUT

Extending a portion of an aluminum foil in a cutting mat. Without removing the blade from the casing, cut a simple design on the foil. This sharpening the edge and remove paper particles or stuck on the sheet vinyl. This can be used for any type of cutting blade.

For heavy-duty cleaning, should be squeezed a sheet of foil on a ball. It is necessary to remove the blade housing of the machine to use this method. Then press the

Plunger, making the sheet and paste into the aluminum foil ball repeatedly. You can do this 50 times. This will make it sharper and also remove particles vinyl or paper sheet.

. . .

How to save your blade

The best way to store the cutting blade is left in the compartment Cricut. It can be placed in the drop-down door that is in front of the machine. This compartment is intended for storing the sheet.

The blade's case can be placed in the plastic points raised in the back of the machine. There are magnets on the front of the computer where you can paste loose sheets.

When you put your sheets on the Cricut machine, never loses its blades.

Cricut Design Space software For Cricut Joy

Moving on to Creating Your Project Template

On the home page, select "New Project", followed by a page with a blank canvas that looks like the grid on your Cricut mats. The words "empty canvas" is a nightmare in itself to any artist, so please just bear with me since we will fill that bad boy up in a second. But first, let's go through the menu options.

New, Templates, Projects, Images, Text, Shapes, and Upload. These are the things that you will see on your left-hand side when you have the canvas open on the screen.

New

New means that you will start a new project and clicking the tab will redirect you to a blank canvas. Be sure to save all changes on your current project before you go to the new canvas. Otherwise, you will lose all of the progress you have already made on that design.

. . .

TEMPLATES

Clicking on Templates will allow you to set a template to help you visualize and work with sizing. It is very handy for someone who is not familiar with Cricut joy Design Space and doesn't know what sizes to set. If you are cutting out wearable items on fabric, you can change the template's size to fit whoever will be wearing it. I'm sure you can agree that this feature is especially beneficial for the seamstresses out there.

PROJECTS

Meanwhile, projects will lead you to the ready-to-make projects so that you can start cutting right away. Some of the projects are not customizable, but others are when you open the template, which is pretty cool. Many of these are not free either, which irks me to a new extent. You can choose the "Free for Cricut (whatever machine you have)", and the projects that will turn up won't have to be paid for.

TEXT

The Text goes without saying. When you select this option, you can type whatever you want and scale it onto your canvas. You may select any font saved in your computer too; that's why collecting those has never been more useful! There is also an option called "multi-layered font", which gives your text a shadow layer. If you are cutting out the letters and shadow layers, the Cricut will do them separately and combine the two later if you wish to. It can create very cool effects so make sure you try that option out. Furthermore, remember that when you are being paid to do a job, the font you are using might require a license to use.

SHAPES

Shapes lets you add basic forms to your canvas, which you can tweak to fit your own needs. The shapes include circle, square, rectangle, triangle, et cetera.

CRICUT BASIC

This is a program or software designed to help the new user get an easy start designing new crafts and DIY projects. This system will help you with image selection to cutting with the least amount of time spent in the design stages. You can locate your image, pre-set projector font, and immediately print, cut, score, and align with tools found within the program. You can use this program on the iOS 7.1.2 or later systems and iPad and several of the iPhones from the Mini to the 5th generation iPod touch. Since it is also a cloud- based service, you can start in one device and finish from another.

CRICUT SYNC

You just connect your system to the computer and run the synced program to install updates on the features that come with your machine. This is also used to troubleshoot many issues that could arise from the hardware.

PLAY AROUND AND PRACTICE

You can combine your shapes and images, add some text, and create patterns. The possibilities are endless. The best thing to do is familiarize yourself with the software before you attempt on cutting expensive materials. Start small and cheap - printer paper will be an ideal choice - and cut away. See what works well for you and stick with it. There are many options concerning the Cricut Design Space. The only way to learn all of this is to experiment and click on every tab you see and try different combinations of options when playing around on the software.

· · ·

MAKING YOUR FIRST PROJECT IDEA

According to the instruction, there will be directions on your screen that you must follow to create your first project after setting up your Cricut joy machine. You will still be using the link you found on the paper when you were setting up your machine. If you have not yet received your machine and are interested in knowing how it works, or you are looking for extra clarifications, here's what it will say.

FIRST STEP

First off, load a pen into the accessories clamp. You can pick whichever color you think will go best with the paper you have received. Next, you want to turn the knob so that the indicator is pointed to "cardstock," considering that is what you will be working with. Have you had a proper look at your mats yet? The blue mat is what you will want to use for this project. You should remove the plastic cover - keep it, don't throw it away as you will need to recover your mat when you're done to avoid dust accumulation - and lay down the paper on the mat with the top left corners of the material and the grid aligned.

SECOND STEP

Make sure that the paper is pressed flat before you push it between the rollers firmly. The mat has to rest on the bottom roller. When it is in place, press the "Load" button to load your mat between the rollers. Press the "go" button, which will be flashing at this stage, and wait for the machine to work its magic on your project. Once everything is done, the light will flash, and you can press the "Load" button again to unload the mat. Your paper will still be sticking to the mat when you remove it.

THIRD STEP

Be careful when removing the material from the mat. Don't be too hasty; take your time so that it doesn't tear. Pull the mat away from the cardstock instead of doing it the other way around. After completing that step, you can now fold the cardstock in half, insert the liners into the corner slots of the card, and it's done!

You have just made your first ever Cricut project in a matter of minutes from start to finish! Congratulations! What are you waiting for? Do more projects! There are a ton of templates you can play around with—practice, practice, practice.

Always keep in mind when starting a new project that you must first have all of the materials necessary to complete the project. It is always helpful to check your stock of tools and materials before getting started. The worst feeling is when you sit down and begin working on a problematic project only to realize you are out of a specific material needed to finish the job. It will save you a lot of time in the long run if you spend a few minutes at the beginning taking stock of your inventory! Working with materials you already have on hand is also a great way to keep your crafting costs low. It will always feel good to know that you made a custom piece of work without spending a ton of extra money just to complete it!

HOW TO UPLOAD IMAGES WITH A CRICUT JOY

For this method to operate, you will need to upload a picture from your desktop. Click complicated once you upload it, and the next window is where the magic takes place.

At the left corner of the top. Look at the wand? Click on it and press on the hair. Click on the continuation button and name the picture. Click the save button.

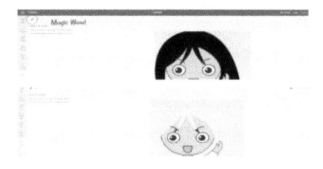

It's gone, and it's been so simple. Now, let's look after her flesh. First press back on the magic wand to remove the face, arms, body, and any hard-to-reach pieces. Once you've finished that, take the eraser to wash the remainder of your flesh until it's gone.

Click Continue, identify your picture, and then press Save when the image is to your liking.

Insert both pictures into the surface of your Cricut Design Space. You can bring them back together once you've got them there. One reason I'm excited about this process is that sometimes, like the hair color, I want to change things. I couldn't change the hair color if I left the picture like it was. But I can do that now.

WOULD YOU LIKE TO KNOW HOW TO EDIT IMAGES IN CRICUT DESIGN SPACE AS THRILLED AS I AM? I pray so

MIKE DAWSON

Now, go out and do some crafting!

Cut Vinyl with a Cricut Joy

Before cutting, ensure that your Circuit joy machine is set to the right setting to cut vinyl. You can select a thin vinyl setting or set the cut to a thicker level, just to ensure that the Cricut joy machine cuts through the vinyl on the first go-round. You will want to back to stay intact, however (this will make weeding a lot easier when you get to this in the next stop) so don't overdo the cut pressure once you are secure in your vinyl placement on the mat, as well as your machine setting, you are ready to go! Once the mat is loaded and the cut button on your Cricut joy Machine is blinking, you are ready to hit the button and begin cutting. Design Space will give you a percentage as to how far into the project it has cut.

How to Make Stickers

How to Make Safari Animal Sticker

Supplies needed are as follows:

- Cricut machine
- Printable sticker paper
- Inkjet prints

Follow the next few steps to create this sticker:

- Load your Cricut design space page and start a new project.
- Click on Upload Images and upload the images of the animal you want. This is an image gotten online.

- Highlight the whole image and use the Flatten button to solidify the image as a whole.
- Resize the image to the appropriate size you desire. You do the residence by clicking on the image, then drag the right side of the box to the size you desire.
- Click Save at the top left to save your project. Save it to be a print and cut image, after which you click the Make It button at the right hand of the screen.
- Examine the end result and make necessary adjustment where you deem it fit. Click Continue after the adjustment. This will lead you to print the design onto the sticker paper.
- Adjust the dial settings on the Cricut machine to the required settings.
- Set the sticker paper on the cutting mat.
- Load the cutting mat into the machine, and push it against the rollers.
- Press the Load/Unload button and then the Go button to cut the stickers.

HOW TO MAKE VINYL STICKER CAR WINDOW

Supplies needed are as follows:

- Cricut machine
- Premium outdoor glossy vinyl
- Transfer tape
- Scraper tool

Follow these steps to create:

- Get and save the image you want to use online.
- Log in to the Cricut design space and start a new project.
- Click on the Upload icon and upload the saved image.
- Click on the image and drag to the next page, then select image type.

- Select the parts of the image you do not want as part of the final cut.
- Select the image as a cute image. You will get to preview the image as a cut image.
- Approve the cut image. You would be redirected to the first upload screen.
- Click on your just finished cut file, then highlight it and insert the image.
- The image is added to your design space for size readjusting. The image is ready to cut.
- Cut the image, and remove excessive vinyl after the image is cut.
- Apply a layer of transfer tape to the top of the cut vinyl.
- Clean the car window really well with rubbing alcohol to remove all dirt.
- Carefully peel away the paperback of the vinyl.
- Apply the cut vinyl on the window. Start at one end and roll it down.
- Go over the applied vinyl with a scraper tool to remove air bubble underneath the vinyl.
- Slowly peel away the transfer tape from the window.

STEPS FOR MAKING ICE-CREAM STICKERS

The supplies needed for this are as follows:

- Cricut machine
- Printable sticker paper
- Inkjet printer

Steps to making an ice-cream sticker:

- Log in to the Cricut design spaces.
- Start a new project and click on the Images at the screen's left side. Select the ice-cream image(s) you want.

- Highlight the whole image and use the Flatten button to solidify the image as one whole piece.
- Resize the image to the appropriate size you need. You realize this by clicking on the image then dragging the right side of the box to the size you desire.
- Click Save at the top left to save your project. Save it to be a print and cut image, after which you click the Make It button at the right hand of the screen.
- Examine the result and click Continue if it's what you expected. This will lead you to print the design onto the paper.
- Adjust the dial on the Cricut machine to the required settings.
- Place the sticker paper on the cutting mat.
- Load the cutting mat into the machine, and push it against the rollers.
- Press the Load/Unload button and then the Go button to cut the stickers.
- Sit back and let the machine print out your designed sticker.

WORKING WITH IMAGES/EDIT PANEL

Have you tried to find out how to edit pictures in the layout room of Cricut? Also me. Usually

EDITING IMAGES IN CRICUT JOY USING THE SLICE TOOL

To assist me in editing pictures in the Cricut Design Space, I used the Slice device. I'm likely still going to use that method for photos I've already uploaded to Cricut Design Space. Let me explain how to edit images using the Slice tool.

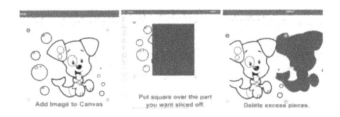

Add Image to Canvas | Put square over the part you want sliced off. | Delete excess pieces.

CLICK ON THE PICTURE AND THEN CLICK INSERT IMAGES TO ADD your attached picture to your Cricut joy canvas. You can add more than one image to your canvas at a time.

Make your picture a lot larger so you can work on it by pressing and pulling it down a little bit on the right upper corner. Just far enough to be able to see it better.

Unlock the table by pressing below the square on the left upper panel. Do you see the icon of the lock? Click on that. Now, using the right top corner, you can transfer the square in any form you want. I placed the circle over the portion that I was about to wipe out, the dog.

Clicking or highlighting the circle, click and hold the change key on your keyboard. Click the picture of the bubble with your mouse, well, bubble for me. This emphasizes both of them.

Click the Slice device at the right upper corner with both the circle and the picture outlined.

Start taking back your slice's parts. There ought to be three parts. They can be deleted.

Continue this method until the manner you want your picture to be printed.

CRICUT SCRAPBOOKING

Scrapbooking is a technique of preserving memories that has existed for quite a while and has developed a lot. In past times, the development of one scrapbook was a monumentally outrageous job.

However, with the creation of products like the Cricut cutting machine, things are a lot easier. If you are looking into developing a scrapbook, this poor boy will be the tool for you. You will find lots of great Cricut suggestions in this book that you can make the most of.

Scrapbooks are simply several of the numerous Cricut suggestions. This tool, in case you know the way to maximize it can enable you to make things go beyond scrapbooking like calendars.

If you purchase a Cricut cartridge, you will find a load of designs uploaded in each one. These pre-created themes are usually utilized for a wide range of items like hangings for walls, picture frames, and greeting cards for those seasons.

Just your imagination is going to limit your progress with a Cricut piece of equipment. With calendars, you can design every month to reflect special events, the mood, and the weather which are associated with it.

The Cricut device can handle that. But in the event that an individual cartridge doesn't keep design which needs, you can constantly go and purchase. It is that simple!

Cricut devices could be a bit costly with the price beginning at ıdoları 299. That is hefty for anyone to begin with. Be a sensible customer. You can often turn to the web to search for deals that are great on Cricut machines.

Everything now appears to be extremely convenient. Should you look for labor now, the majority has become machine intensive instead of labor-intensive. It doesn't mean suggesting that today, leave the machines and allow them to perform the work.

They nevertheless need the working prowess of individuals. I never wish it involves that time where devices are self - operating.

The art of scrapbook making is but one facet of human civilization, which has become a lot easier due to engineering merchandise, especially the Cricut cutting machine. It is at this time which Cricut scrapbooking takes the center stage.

In case you are considering of putting in the Cricut scrapbooking world, this device is a must-have. You cannot say no and just claim that I can do it by hand because doing this will drive you to the cliff and into the jaws of insanity.

Utilizing Shape Cartridge helps you develop shapes like animals, tags, boxes, dolls, and hearts amongst others. Pick these cutout symbols to embellish your scrapbook for a fascinating remembrance on your own or a present for someone very special.

SOLVING THE MOST COMMON PROBLEM WHEN USING CRICUT JOY

DOES THE CRICUT MAKER CUT FABRIC PATTERNS SUCH AS CLOTHES, pants, shirts, skirts, blouses etc.?

Absolutely Yes, the Cricut Machine can cut through fabric patterns the Cricut Maker comes with 25 patters for sewing to assist you to get started. In addition the Cricut Maker comes with hundreds of design patterns in collaboration with Simplicity.

DOES THE CRICUT MAKER ETCH THROUGH GLASS?

Yes, the Cricut maker can etch glass but not directly. To do this you need to create and cut your own design patterns using the Design space and applying an etching cream onto the glass surface.

DO I LOSE MY PROJECTS, UPLOADED IMAGES AND CARTRIDGES when upgrading the Cricut Maker?

No. Your projects, cartridges and uploaded images remain intact the reason being because you typically use a Cricut ID in the Cricut cloud and not machines with the same Cricut ID and not the machine itself. So you can be sure all you content will be accessible with the Cricut Maker.

DOES THE CRICUT MAKER ENGRAVE METALLIC MATERIALS SUCH AS JEWELLERY OR PET ID TAGS?

Yes, but to technically achieve this you need a special etching tool for it to go through a third party. This is because the deep engraving functionality may fail on some metallic objects. Among such tools you may need is an etching tool by "Chomas creation" which fits into the Cricut Maker as other tools. With the tool, you can engrave or etch material such as leather, metal clay, silver, aluminum, bronze, copper, plastic, and acrylic

DO I NEED A PRINTER? WHAT PRINTER SHOULD I USE?

Absolutely No, Cricut joy machines are not dependent upon printers.

As far as what printer to get, you just need something that prints color! Some of the most versatile Hp machine is the HP Envy, but there are many great printers out there in the market that are not limited to Hp.

Does there exist any difference in the power Cords of the Cricut joy Machine?

No, there is a physical difference in the Power cords of the Cricut joy Machines. However, there is a difference in the output current with the Cricut joy cord upgraded to supply 3A with its predecessors— Cricut Explore having a 2.5A output current supply. This adaption also allows you to charge your mobile phone via its charging port on the right-hand side while multitasking the cutting/writing functionalities.

However if you using the Cricut Explore you can still charge the mobile phone device. Still, the difference is that because of its low current capacity it will either slow, stutter or even shut off (in extreme cases) because the device will need a current supply and the cutting operation —which needs more current supply especially as it requires more cutting pressure.

WHAT MATERIALS CAN I CUT USING THE CRICUT JOY?

The Cricut engineering team is in the process of experimenting more materials, cutting pressures and guidelines. However the following are some of the materials it cuts; fabric, papers—crepe and tissue, vinyl, cardstock, cork, leather, duct tape, faux leather, chipboard, felt, adhesive foil, among others.

HOW DOES THE ROTARY CUTTER DIFFER WITH THE FABRIC blade?

The Cricut Maker can use both, the rotary blade, and the bonded fabric blade. However the difference is that the rotary blade can cut through delicate materials without a backing material. In contrast, the rotary blade will need to use the Adaptive tool system to perform the precision cutting experience.

WHAT IS THE PINK MAT AND HOW CAN I USE IT?

The Pink Mat is useful for cutting fabrics as well as other delicate materials. It is highly durable therefore strong which means it can withstand pressure when cutting thin materials. You may be asking how it needs a strong material whereas the material under cut is thin. It takes a lot of pressure when cutting delicate materials meaning it needs to stay flat on the mat to resist the need to shift.

ARE BLADES AND TOOLS OF THE CRICUT JOY AND OTHER PREDECESSORS INTERCHANGEABLE?

Yes and No. The tools of the Cricut joy cannot be used in the Cricut

Explore machines however the blades of the Cricut Maker can be used by the Cricut Explore machines. Simply the reason being the Cricut joy came after the Cricut Explore therefore the functionalities of the Cricut Explore differ with that the Cricut joy with the latter being more advanced compared to the Explore. It does not have the drive gears that control the rotary blade and knife, for starters, and the pressure required to operate these tools are simply not present in the Explore.

HOW DOES THE CRICUT JOY DIFFER WITH ITS PREDECESSORS IN TERMS OF THE SOFTWARE?

Both are similar in terms of software because they use the Cricut Design space. This means that all the Explore projects can be cut by the Cricut joy whereas some project by Cricut Maker can be also be cut by the Cricut Explore as long as it does not concern the rotary and knife blades.

FAQs about the Cricut Maker & Joy

Why does Design Space say my Cricut machine is already in use when it's not?

To resolve this, make sure that you've completed the New Machine Setup for your Cricut. Try Design Space in another browser. The two that work best are Google Chrome and Mozilla Firefox; if it doesn't work in one of those, try the other. If that doesn't clear the error, try a different USB port and USB cable. Disconnect the machine from the computer and turn it off. While it's off, restart your computer. After your computer restarts, reconnect the machine and turn it on. Wait a few moments, and then try Design Space again. If you're still having the same problem, contact Cricut Member Care.

Why doesn't my cut match the preview in Design Space?

Test another image and see if the same thing happens. If it's only happening with the one project, create a new project and start over or try a different image. If it happens with a second project, and your machine is connected with Bluetooth, disconnect that and plug it in with a USB cable. Larger projects may sometimes have difficulty communicating the cuts over Bluetooth. If you can't connect with USB or the problem is still occurring, check that your computer matches or exceeds the running Design Space system requirements. If it doesn't, try the project on a different computer or mobile device that does. If your computer does meet the requirements, open Design Space in a different browser and try again. If the problem continues, try a different USB cable. Finally, if the issue still hasn't resolved, contact Cricut Member Care.

WHAT DO I DO IF I NEED TO INSTALL USB DRIVERS FOR MY Cricut machine?

TYPICALLY, THE CRICUT DRIVERS ARE AUTOMATICALLY INSTALLED when you connect it with a USB cable. If Design Space doesn't see your machine, you can try this to troubleshoot the driver installation. First, open Device Manager on your computer. You'll need to have administrator rights. For Windows 7, click Start, right-click on Computer, and select Manage.

WHY DOES MY CRICUT MAKER SAY THE BLADE IS NOT DETECTED?

MAKE SURE THAT THE TOOL IN CLAMP B IS THE SAME ONE DESIGN Space recommends in the Load Tools step of the Project Preview screen. If you don't have that recommended tool, unload your mat and select Edit Tools on the Project Preview screen. Here, you can select a different tool. If the tool and the selection already match, carefully remove the tool from Clamp B and clean the reflective band on the housing. Reinstall it in the clamp and press the Go button. If that doesn't resolve the problem, remove the tool again and clean the machine's sensor. Reinstall the tool and press Go again.

WHY IS MY CRICUT MACHINE MAKING A GRINDING NOISE?

IF IT'S THE CARRIAGE CAR MAKING A LOUD NOISE AFTER YOU PRESS the cut button, and it sounds like the carriage might be hitting the side of the machine, record a short video of it and send it to Cricut Member Care. If the noise comes from a brand-new machine the first time you use it, contact Cricut Member Care. Otherwise, make sure that you're using the original power cord that came with your machine. If the machine isn't getting the correct voltage, it may produce a grinding sound. If you are using the machine's power cord, adjust your pressure settings. If it's too high, it might produce an unusual sound. Decrease it in increments of 2–4, and do some test cuts. If it's still making the issue even after decreasing the cutting pressure, contact Cricut Member Care.

WHY IS MY MAT GOING INTO THE MACHINE CROOKED?

CHECK THE ROLLER BAR TO SEE IF IT'S LOOSE, DAMAGED, OR UNEVEN. If it is, take a photo or video of it to send to Cricut Member Care. If the roller bar seems fine, make sure that you're using the right mat size for the machine. Make sure the mat is correctly lined up with the guides and that the edge is underneath the roller bar when you prepare to load it. If it's still loading crookedly even when properly lined up with the guides, try applying gentle pressure to the mat to get it under the roller bar once it starts. If none of this works, contact Cricut Member Care.

. . .

WHY ISN'T THE SMART SET DIAL CHANGING THE MATERIAL IN DESIGN SPACE?

MAKE SURE THAT THE USB CABLE BETWEEN THE COMPUTER AND THE CRICUT EXPLORE IS PROPERLY CONNECTED. If so, disconnect the Explorer from the computer and turn it off. Restart your computer. Once it's on, turn on the Explore, plug it into the computer, and try the cut again. If it still isn't changing the material, connect the USB cable to a different port on the computer. If it's still not working, try Design Space in multiple web browsers and see if the problem replicates. If it does, try an entirely different USB cable. Check for Firmware Updates for the Explore. If you don't have another USB cable, the Firmware Update doesn't help, or there are no Firmware Updates, contact Cricut Member Care.

WHAT DO I DO IF MY CRICUT MAKER STOPPED PARTWAY through a cut?

IF THE KNIFE BLADE STOPS CUTTING AND THE GO BUTTON ARE flashing, the Maker has encountered some error. In Design Space, you'll get a notification that the blade is stuck. This might have been caused by the blade running into something like a knot or seam if too much dust or debris built up in the cut area or if the blade got into a gouge in the mat from a previous cut. To resume your project, do not unload the mat. This will lose your place in the project, and it will be impossible to get it lined up again. Check the cut area for dust or debris, and gently clean it.

WHY IS MY FABRIC GETTING CAUGHT UNDER THE ROLLERS?

BE SURE TO CUT DOWN ANY FABRIC SO THAT IT FITS ON YOUR MAT

without going past the adhesive. If you have stuck the fabric and realize it's hanging past the adhesive, use a ruler and a sharp blade to trim it. Or, if it's the correct size but slightly askew, unstick it and reposition it.

WHY WOULD MY CRICUT MAKER CONTINUOUSLY TURN OFF DURING CUTS?

THIS CAN HAPPEN FROM A BUILD-UP OF STATIC ELECTRICITY WHILE cutting foil and metal sheets. Makers in dry areas are more susceptible to this. Spritzing water in the air will dissipate the build-up. Be careful not to spray any water directly on the Maker. Using a humidifier or vaporizer in the area where you use your Maker can help avoid the static build-ups. If this doesn't seem to be what's causing the issue, contact Cricut Member Care.

Tips that might Assist You To Begin

If you can you can subscribe to the access for about ten dollars a month to gain access to over twenty thousand different images and over a thousand different projects. You even get over three hundred fonts.

You will also need to keep the plastic sheets that come with the mats to protect them between your uses.

Clean your cutting mats with baby wipes that are water-based to keep them sticky and clean longer.

Use one blade for your cardstock and a separate one for vinyl because this will let them both last longer.

MAKE SURE THAT YOU HAVE A DEEP CUT BLADE.

This is for people who have had the cartridges for an older machine or older cartridge. You can hook these up to your new account. It is a simple thing to do but you should know that you could only link them once so be sure that if you are buying a machine second hand, nothing has been linked yet.

The right tools are important here so you should make sure that you have the toolset. It will contain vital tools that you need, and they can especially help with vinyl.

KNOW YOUR GLUE

Many people are huge fans of what is called tacky glue. It gives your projects a little bit of wiggle room when you're trying to position them. The problem is that it can take longer to dry. If this is something that bothers you, you might want to try a quicker one. Zip dry paper glue it's extremely sticky and much faster.

A tip that will go along with the tip above is that you want them to be a layer to pop out from another layer. You can make this happen by using products like pop dots or Zots. They are self-adhesive foam mounts. You can also make little circles using craft foam or cardboard and then glue it between the layers.

THINK ABOUT A COACH

Business mentors are extremely popular nowadays. Consider going through some cash with a Scrapbooking business mentor who comprehends the business as well as genuinely comprehends the specific brand of energy scrapbook sweethearts share. A mentor can help share business abilities however can go about as an extraordinary coach in managing you to your objectives.

EXHIBIT YOUR TRUE TALENT WITH A BUSINESS CARD FOR Artists

The financial downturn has left huge numbers of us feeling the squeeze. Numerous individuals are searching for approaches to set aside cash in each part of life. Be that as it may, there are times when a buy must be made, and cautious research regularly structures some portion of the basic leadership the procedure.

. . .

GIVE THE QUALITY OF YOUR WORK A CHANCE TO RADIATE through

A business card for specialists is your window to the world, and it should say a great deal regarding your aesthetic edge and abilities. Make it state every little thing about you and what you can offer. Plan a motivating logo that can join the substance of what you can do with an incredible structure. This astute connecting can put you on top of things by helping individuals to recollect who and what you are.

CONSIDER OTHER WAYS YOU CAN DISPLAY YOUR SKILLS TO the World

A business card for specialists is only one of numerous limited time apparatuses you can use to enhance your presentation. It bodes well. The production of a notice is a magnificent method to demonstrate the best of what you do. Try not to place a lot into your sign; that will go about as an obstacle and prevent individuals from getting a vibe of your actual abilities. Consider the area where you can show your blurb. Vital arranging of the setting of your sign can help augment its effect. It will expand the intrigue of your work and open up more potential outcomes.

REMEMBER TO TELL INDIVIDUALS HOW TO CONNECT!

A business card for specialists needs not exclusively to demonstrate the embodiment of your innovativeness; it likewise fills a need. It needs to tell potential clients how to connect with you. Incorporate all the distinctive contact techniques you have, email, site, telephone numbers, and any online networking you are an individual from. Remember the intensity of internet based life and bookmarking destinations; they can enable feature to considerably a greater amount of your work.

. . .

BE ADAPTABLE

Consider chipping away at zones that you hadn't imagined, however will be something inside your abilities. This will enable you to set up notoriety. Another viable method to advance your aptitudes notwithstanding utilizing a business card for specialists is to engage in network ventures where you offer your administrations for nothing. Make something stunning that individuals will see every day; this is an incredible advert for your aptitudes. This will place your work into thousands of individuals' lives and drive more clients to you.

Conclusion

In this book, we have given you the tools to make your Cricut work at its best all day every day. When you can do this, you will be able to make anything that you want because these machines can cut amazingly well and they have so many functions that it could make your head spin. This book has been able to help you see the difference between the different machines and how and why the prices are different. Each machine has something that it does best and the Maker is the best of the four as it can cut more than any other machine. This means that you get to work with new materials that you will not use with the other machines because they can't cut it. They call the Maker the ultimate machine because it can do what others can't.

When you choose the machine that will work best with you, you will find that the website from the company itself is much cheaper than the other retailers that you can find online. The benefit from buying from the company itself is that you do not have to deal with a third party. Instead, you get coupons, bundles and discounts that you are looking for, and there is no problem with the machine. In addition to that, when you buy from a third party retailer, they do not let you bundle at all so you will be paying an extra per item you want. This can get very expensive very quickly.

We also give you great advice on projects that you can do with your particular machine. There are somethings that individual devices can cut and others can't cut very much. If you are doing heavy-duty projects, you will need a machine that can do this. This is why we have compiled the best information for you.

Thank you for downloading this book!!

CRICUT EXPLORE AIR 2

How To Master The Cricut Machine In No Time With Easy Step-By-Step Illustrations, Tips, Tricks And Much More

Introduction

The Cricut Explore Air 2 can be regarded as an electronic cutter or a personal crafting machine which can be used in the cutting of different materials such as the cardstock, vinyl, Faux leather, Magnet sheets, sticker paper, Vellum, Fabric, Sticker Paper, etc.

The Cricut Explore Air 2 can make use of the pen and markers in writing, drawing as well as scoring your project with a nifty score tool. The machine can also be used in printing and cutting, as well.

One unique thing about Cricut Explore Air 2 is that its tools are made of high quality and has two cutting modes: fast and normal modes, to deliver your project with precision.

The Cricut Explore Air 2 is an electronic cutting machine that makes use of a precise blade as well as series of rollers in cutting out images, just anything you can imagine. It is used in cutting out fancy paper shapes as well as fonts that came on cartridges.

CHAPTER 1: WHAT IS CRICUT MACHINE

What is Cricut?

Cricut is a brand name for a variety of products referred to as home die cutting machines. These machines are used for scrapbooking and other countless creative projects. Cricut is one of the most popular among several electronic die cutters used by scrapbookers, paper crafters, and card makers. Cricut machines are designed to cut paper, vinyl, felt, balsa wood, and various types of fabrics. The Cricut logo is a play on an animated cricket bug, which the name closely represents. The Cricut logo is used throughout their different design offerings, including Cricut Design Space, and Cricut Access.

When the Cricut was introduced, it gave crafters all over the world a long sought-after tool for Do It Yourself project in a new, fun, and innovative way. It gave people a new opportunity to approach their projects and creativity. Cricut now influences passion and originality in a way that people truly enjoy! People all over the world have been able to make successful businesses from their Cricut design which brings more and more people to the world of Cricut crafting each and every year. Now is the perfect time to get started using the Circuit machine if this is something you want to obtain for yourself, and this book will help you get there.

Cricut Machine Models

There are various Cricut models to look over. In the event that you are planning to buy a Cricut to use at home or for your business at that point let this Cricut machines examination help you out.

- **Cricut Maker**

The Cricut Maker is Circuits' most up to date machine. Cricut considers it a definitive smart cutting machine, and I can't help but agree. It is a best in class digital die the cutting machine that conveys proficient quality outcomes at an individual machine cost. It can cut many materials, from the most delicate fabric and paper to mat board, balsa wood, and leather.

The Cricut Maker utilizes the fresh out of the box new Adaptive Tool System, which takes into account progressively precise control over the instruments, including pivoting, lifting, and shifting weight all through the whole cut. The Adaptive Tool System also enables the machine to use new kinds of devices later on as Cricut grows its device contributions.

Other than the Fine-Point Blade, Deep Cut Blade, and Bonded Fabric

Blade that are good with all Cricut machines, the Maker can also utilize the accompanying apparatuses that are perfect with the Adaptive Tool System:

Rotating Blade – This gives you a chance to cut fabric with a Cricut Maker and it's a tremendous improvement over-utilizing the standard Fine-Point cutting edge. You can cut intense fabric like burlap or denim, and furthermore delicate materials like crepe paper or glossy silk. This cutting edge gives you a chance to make intricate cuts on fabric without fraying or clustering (which is the reason you need a stabilizer backing when utilizing the Fine-Point blade).

This lets you effectively cut through thicker and denser materials, for example, balsa wood, leather, mat board, and Cricut Chipboard. You can make some quite complex cuts without worrying that the sharp edge will snap.

Scoring Wheels

These apparatuses make crisp creases on slender, thick, and even covered paper materials. They enable you to make extra-deep score lines on any material that doesn't break when you fold it.

The Explore machines can't utilize these new sharp edges and instruments since they depend on the Adaptive Tool System. The standard instrument holder carriage in the Explore machines simply doesn't have the necessary exactness or power.

As the name suggests, the Adaptive Tool System is intended to easily switch between devices, adjusting the drive framework to whichever device is loaded into it. This considers TONS of new kinds of instruments to be made, later on, to do new sorts of arts with the machine that we never could. I think the Adaptive Tool System is a HUGE advantage and I think it makes the Maker increasingly "future-verification"; I suspect we'll see a huge amount of cool new devices for the Adaptive Tool System soon!

Features

With expandable devices: revolving cutting edge, pens, and knife blade

With fine point pen, 12 x 12 inches cutting mats

The rotational cutting edge can cut quickly and precisely

Accompanies several computerized sewing designs

The knife blade can deal with meager and thick materials

With simple structure application; load extends on a PC or cell phon e

With a gadget docking space

You can utilize your own plans

With a USB port to charge your gadget while being used

With Bluetooth remote innovation

Pros

Enables you to work at various materials

You can utilize various structures from its database

Accompanies expandable devices

Gadget dock gives you a chance to work intimately with the machine

Utilize your PC or cell phone with the Cricut

Cons

Objections that it won't work with an iPad

The blade edge is sold independently

- **Cricut Explore Air**

THE CRICUT EXPLORE AIR IS THE SUBSEQUENT STAGE UP FROM THE EXPLORE ONE. It also comes the standard Fine-Point Blade which enables you to cut several materials, and it's good with the Deep Point Blade and the Bonded Fabric Blade (sold independently) to enable you to cut considerably more materials.

One major redesign over the Explore One is that the Cricut Explore Air has a double apparatus holder; it is intended to hold a cutting edge in one clamp and a pen, scoring stylus, or another embellishment in the other clip. This implies if you have a project that has both writing and cutting, you can stack a sharp edge and a pen into the machine, and it will cut and write across the board go without stopping for you to change between instruments. Far better, the second clasp is perfect with tools like the Scoring Stylus, Cricut Pens, and so on so there's no reason to buy an extra connector .

The Cricut Explore Air also offers worked in Bluetooth abilities. For the initial step, you should associate utilizing the USB link gave, yet after the underlying matching, you'll have the option to interface with your machine and cut remotely.

Features

With double cartridge to cut, compose or score simultaneously

With inserted Bluetooth, so you can work remotely

Will cut in excess of 60 distinct materials

With incorporated stockpiling segments

Good with .svg, .jpg, .png, .bmp, .gif, .dxf documents

Will take a shot at all Cricut cartridges

Pros

Cut and compose, cut and score simultaneously

You can work remotely

Store pens, blades and different frill away compartments

You can utilize your very own pictures or utilize any picture from the tremendous library

Works with Cricut cartridges

Cons

You have to buy extra apparatuses and accessories

You have to buy fonts and designs

- **Cricut Explore Air 2**

THE CRICUT EXPLORE AIR 2 IS THE FOLLOWING STAGE UP FROM THE EXPLORE AIR, and it has one significant update: Fast Mode. This is extremely useful for individuals who make various duplicates of their tasks (like educators) or individuals who make things to sell who will value the measure of time they spare.

The Cricut Explore Air 2 accompanies the standard Fine-Point Blade which enables you to cut several materials, and it's perfect with the Deep Point Blade and the Bonded Fabric Blade (sold independently) to enable you to cut considerably more materials.

The Cricut Explore Air 2 additionally has worked in Bluetooth abilities so you can cut remotely and a double tool holder so you can cut and compose all in a solitary pass. Furthermore, similar to the Explore Air, the second clamp is good with frill like the Scoring Stylus, Cricut Pens, and so on so there's no compelling reason to buy an extra connector.

Personally, I don't really utilize Fast Mode all that frequently, so the progression up from the Explore Air is definitely not a huge deal for me, however, it can spare you time if you do a ton of cardstock, vinyl, and iron-on projects!

Features

With Cricut Pens to make "written by hand" cards and different projects

Cut multifaceted subtleties with extreme exactness

With Scoring Stylus to crease cards, boxes, envelopes, acetic acid derivation and to make 3D paper specialties

With Fast Mode for 2X quicker cutting

You can work with more than 100+ sorts of material s

Within excess of 370 textual styles to look over

Can work with an Android or iOS gadget

Remote cutting with Bluetooth

Utilizations Design Space to deal with records from any gadget

With Cricut Image Library

Pros

Scoring Stylus folds lines for various projects

Cuts with extreme accuracy

Works with more than 100+ materials

Writes more than 370 text styles

Structure anyplace with Design Space

Associates with gadgets by means of Bluetooth

Cut and write multiple times quicker

Cons

Issues with Design Space

Disconnected Design Space accessible for iOS clients

- **Cricut Explore One**

THE CRICUT EXPLORE ONE IS CIRCUITS' ENTRANCE LEVEL SPENDING machine; it's ideal for any individual who needs to begin with a digital die cutting machine yet wouldn't like to spend a huge amount of cash. It accompanies the standard Fine-Point Blade which enables you to cut several materials, and it's perfect with the Deep Point Blade and the Bonded Fabric Blade (sold independently) to enable you to cut considerably more materials.

As its name suggests, the Explore One has a single apparatus holder, so if you need to cut and write in a similar project you should change out the sharp edge for a pen mid-route through the cut. It's extremely simple to change out the accessory or blade, and the Design Space programming will stop the slice and walk you through it when now is the right time, yet if you do a lot of tasks that join cutting, composing, or scoring, it can get tiresome sooner or later.

Moreover, really, the single tools holder is good with the standard estimated edges (Fine-Point, Deep Point, and Bonded Fabric), however, to utilize different instruments and extras, you'll have to buy a different connector to fit in the single device holder.

The Explore One doesn't have worked in Bluetooth capacities, so you need to connect the machine to your gadget with the USB link gave. Or then again you can buy a Bluetooth connector independently to enable the machine to cut remotely.

Features

Utilize the Cricut Design Space for PC, Mac, iPad or iPhone

Transfer your own plans for nothing or pick one from the Cricut Image Librar y

Use text styles introduced from your PC

Work on various materials from flimsy paper to thick vinyl

With helpful device and extras holder

Works remotely by including a remote Bluetooth connector

No compelling reason to set with the Smart Set dial or make your very own custom settings

Make extends in minutes

Pros

Works remotely with Bluetooth connector

Transfer your very own pictures and structures for nothing

With 50,000+ pictures and text styles from Cricut Image Library

No settings required with the Smart Set dial

Prints and cuts quick

Structure with your very own gadget or PC utilizing Design Space

Cons

It expenses to utilize pictures beginning at $0.99

Bluetooth connector sold independently

- **Cricut Expression 1**

YOU CAN MAKE MORE CUSTOMIZATIONS FOR VARIOUS PROJECTS WITH THE CRICUT EXPRESSION 1. This electronic cutting machine works with the Cricut Craft Room where you can alter plans and improve your output even more. With its six modes and four capacities, you will have the option to make a variety of projects. You can also appreciate quick cutting and plotting speeds which imply that you can make extends quicker, perfect for business use. Expression 1 is additionally portable you can take it any place you should be; at school, at home or at the workplace. It has an LCD screen however touchscreen isn't.

Your buy accompanies a 12" x 12" cutting mat so there is no compelling reason to buy.

The Cricut Expression 1 is portable and woks productively; you can make numerous kinds of activities any way you have to buy cartridges since this one doesn't accompany one. In fact, you can't make any projects yet when this comes out of the box.

Features

Can cut moment 0.25" pictures to 23.5" plans

Will work with the Cricut Craft Room

With ordinary LCD screen

With 6 modes and 4 distinct capacities to improve customization

Buy accompanies a 12" x 12" cutting mat

Compact structure

Cuts rapidly and productively

Pros

Totally adaptable to make better plans

With six modes and four capacities

Accompanies a 12" x 12" cutting mat

Works with Cricut Craft Roo m

With a convenient plan

Cons

Issues with the sticky mat

No cartridges included with buy

Isn't perfect with different cartridges

Cricut Easy Press Machine

- **Cricut Easy Press**

ANOTHER CUTTING MACHINE THAT WORTH IS THE CRICUT EASY Press. I state that it worth the investment due to the home-accommodating structure and star level execution. It accompanies a major handle, a security base, and an auto-shutoff include so as to keep your home, workspace, and office very protected. In the event that you request this workhorse, you will get a compact, lightweight and simple to store with a giant, clay-covered warmth plate that gives the definite temperature you need. It is ideal for layered or enormous iron-on projects. It accompanies a reference diagram that will assist you in deciding time and temperature.

Pros

Ace level execution

Home-accommodating structure

Portable and compact

Reference graph included

Auto-shutoff highlight

Cons

Manual warmth temperature and clock settings

Conflicting weight and little cutting zone

Which Cricut Machine Should You Purchase?

There are 3 versions of this Cricut system, popular private die cutters produced available by the Provo Craft business. With three great possibilities, it can be hard to choose which to purchase. In the event you start little and purchase the first Personal Electronics Cutter? Or is your Expression model value the additional investment? How can the Generate, the hybrid version now being exclusively offered by Michael's Craft Store, stand against both of the other machines?

In numerous ways, all 3 die cut machines will be precisely the same:

- **All three versions are cartridge-based.**

You can only create cutouts depending upon the capsules you possess. Each cartridge includes a computer keyboard overlay, which can be employed in choosing special cuts. The cartridges aren't machine-specific - they may be utilized in any of those 3 versions .

- **Fundamental performance of three machines is exactly the exact same.**

If you have the personal electronic cutter, then you'll not have any trouble working on the Cricut expression or produce (along with vice-versa). Why? The fundamental operation of three die cutters would be exactly the exact same.

Here is a fast rundown of this procedure. After plugging in the chosen cartridge and accompanying computer keyboard overlay and turning to the machine, then you're prepared to begin making die cuts. Materials, like paper or cardstock, are set on a particular cutting edge mat, which is subsequently loaded to the machine using all the press of a switch. With another press on this button, the chosen design is selected. All that is left is to choose "cut". The device does the remainder of the job.

- **All three Cricut machine versions utilize the very same accessories.**

It was mentioned that the capsules aren't machine-specific, but in addition, this is true with the majority of the additional accessories. It isn't important which version you have - that the replacement blades, blades, different instruments, like the Cricut spatula, and design studio applications, may be utilized with almost any version. The 1 exception is that the cutting mats. The machines take various sizes of their mats, and you need to get one that's compatible with your particular machine.

Now that you understand the way the Cricut machines are alike, you're most likely wondering how they're different.

They change in many ways

- **The dimensions of die cuts made by every machine are distinct.**

The personal electronic cutter has the capacity of earning cutouts ranging from 1 inch to 5-1/2 inches in dimension, in half inch increments. The generate can create die cuts that range from 1/4 inch to 11-1/2 inches in dimension, per inch increments. The expression provides users the maximum flexibility, making cutouts out of 1/4 inch to 23-1/2 inches in dimension, per quarter inch increments .

- **They size and weight of these machines change.**

The personal electronic cutter and produce are equally small, mobile machines. These versions are great for crafters who prefer to shoot their jobs on the street and make record layouts and other jobs in class settings. They're also suited for people who don't own a particular place in their house place aside for crafting, since these die cutters are easy to package up and set away between applications. The expression, on the other hand, is considerably heavier and bigger. In case you've got a crafting corner or room, and don't have the worries of transferring it regularly, it is a fantastic option.

- **The three Cricut machine versions have various functions and modes.**

There are many distinct modes and purposes. By way of instance, the match to page style will automatically correct the dimensions of this die cut predicated upon the dimensions of this material loaded from the system. The middle point function lets you align with the cutting blade across the middle of this substance, so the cut is created about it. The expression machine gets the most flexibility so much as the access to functions and modes. Next in line would be the produce, and third place belongs to the personal electronic cutter. More info could be found regarding such functions and modes in the system handbooks, which can be found in pdf format on cricut.com.

- **The cost differs for every version.**

The personal electronic cutter is the most inexpensive Cricut cutter, having an estimated retail price of $299.99. The generate is $100.00 longer, at $399.99, as well as the rake is $499.99. Please be aware that all 3 machines can be bought at substantial savings. Many retailers operate particular sales or possess a lesser regular cost compared to suggested retail cost. It is a fantastic idea to look around when purchasing your very first Cricut machine.

WHAT PROJECTS CAN BE DONE WITH A CRICUT MACHINE?

We cannot talk about all projects that can be done with a Cricut machine because there are so many. However, for all creative minds to enter the guide, here are some of the popular projects that can be done with a Cricut machine.

Creation, custom handmade card s

Cut letters or shapes for scrapbooking. Addressing an envelope.

I am creating a leather bracelet.

Design and creation of decorations or email for holidays. Design and production of Christmas decorations and ornaments. Design t-shirts or other tissues.

Templates are making paint and creating vinyl stickers.

We are creating labels.

Design and creation of symbolic pillows.

Design registration plates, cups, glasses, or cups. Engraved designs on glass.

Creating decorations and stickers for your walls. Creating designs in wood or wood samples.

Cutting pieces of fabric to plant another fabric or quilt squares. Creating decorative stickers.

We are creating mountains of felt.

We are creating designs for water bottles.

Design and creation of custom bags.

CHAPTER 2: MACHINE SETUP AND HOW TO PREPARE THE MATERIAL

Setting up the Cricut Explore Air 2

Once you can set up your Cricut Explore Air 2, it will lead to the automatic registration of the machine to your account. To set up there Cricut Explore Air 2, you will need to take the following steps: - Get the device plugged in and turn it on.

- Make use of the USB cord in connecting or the Bluetooth in pairing the Cricut Explore Air 2 to your computer.

- On the computer, visit design.cricut.com/setup.

- You will be prompted by On-screen instructions to create your Cricut ID and getting signed in.

- When prompted, download and install the Design Space plug-in.

- Once you are prompted to begin your first project, the setup is complete .

Useful Tips

Once you go through this process of getting your machine setup, the machine will be registered automatically.

In a situation where you couldn't go through with the setup when the Cricut was connected to your PC at first, you will need to get the machine reconnected and visit the design portal on the Cricut website, or visit the Design Space Account menu, select New Machine Setup and follow the on-screen instructions that come up.

How to Plug in the Device?

First, the Cricut machine needs to be plugged into the computer and also the power outlet. Use the USB cable provided to connect the computer to the machine. Next to the USB cable, the power port should be connected to both the outlet and the device, also provided in the packaging. Now press the ON button on the machine. It will illuminate to indicate that it is working.

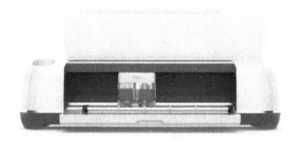

How to Load/Unload the Mat?

For placing your material to cut it on the mat, it's important to know the placement. First, the mat's cover should be removed and placed elsewhere. The Cricut maker comes with a blue LightGrip mat, which is used for cutting paper mainly. The match will be slightly sticky for good placement of the material. When loading, the material should be placed in the top left corner of the mat. Be sure to press down gently so that the material could be evened out.

Place the top of the mat in the guides of the machine. Gently press on the rollers and press the load/to unload the button on top of the Cricut. Once loaded up, the software will tell you the next step. After the project has been finished, the material needs to be unloaded. Press on the load/unload button and take out the mat from the machine. The right way to remove the material from the mat is that it should be placed on a straight surface, and the mat should be peeled off. The remaining scraps can be peeled off by a scrapper or a tweezer.

How to Load/Unload Cricut Pen?

For loading a pen, the machine needs to be opened to show the two clamps. For placement of the pen, clamp A needs to be opened up. Remove the cap on the pen and place it so that the arrow on the pen is facing the front. Gently pull clamp an upwards when placing the pen. Place the pen inside clamp until the arrow disappears, and a click sound is heard. To unload a pen, simply open up clamp A and remove the pen by upward motion. If you do not remove the pen, the machine will not be close, and the pen's cap cannot be put on.

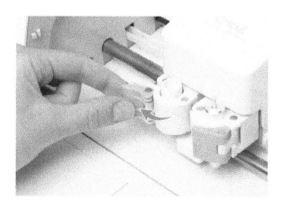

Recently, new specialized pens are available called the Infusible Ink Pen and markers.

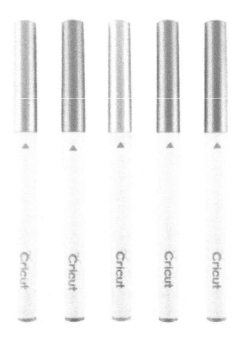

THEY WORK IN BY SUBLIMATION PROCESS, COMPLETELY FUSING THE ink onto the material. It is best for Iron-on. The difference between it and regular pens is that they leave a thicker line. They also come in in two variations: traditional and neon. Heating is required to use this instrument, which can be achieved by Cricut Easy Press. For using it, first select a blank slot and fit in pen, any blank slot can fit the pens. Then draw your design on design space or by hand. Make sure the image size is according to the Cricut Easy Press. Then place a laser paper on to the Cricut Maker or Cricut Explorer. Now use the Infusible Ink to draw in the design. Now transfer the image to Cricut Easy Press and follow its guidelines.

How to Load/Unload Blades?

A Fine point blade comes already place inside the machine when the package is opened. If the project requires a changing of the blade, then first, you need to unload the blade. Open up accessory clamp B and pull it upwards gently. Then pull the blade out of the machine. When putting another blade, i.e., rotary blade, make sure that the gears fit evenly. Once placed, it will give a click sound. Whenever someone is doing a project, the Cricut Maker automatically checks if the right blade is placed. With QuickSwap housing available, it is easier to change blades. Simply press on the housing tip to loosen its grip, and then slide or remove the blades.

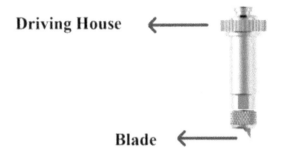

Driving House ⟵

Blade ⟵

How to **unmount the paper from** the mat

- Bend the paper until it pops out a little bit and uses your finger to remove the paper from the mat. You can also use the tools provided to make a little bit easier.

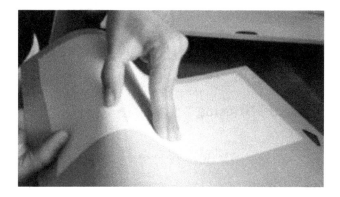

WHEN YOU REMOVE THE PAPER AND FOLD IT THIS IS WHAT YOU should have.

WHEN YOU OPEN IT, YOU WILL FIND A SPACE THAT YOU COULD write your message on.

- Once you get to this stage, you have to head back to the computer and click on continue.

- The computer will keep on guiding you if you want to add more design to the one you have already done.

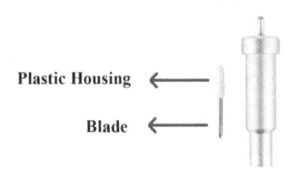

Plastic Housing ⟵

Blade ⟵

How to Load/Unload a Scoring Stylus?

To load and unload a scoring stylus is just as loading and uploading the pen. Open up the accessory clamp A and put the pen tip downwards, while holding up the clamp gently. Place it in until the arrow disappears, and a click sound is made. Now close the clamp and follow the instructions in the software. Once the scoring is completed, the scoring pen needs to be unloaded. Open up the clamp and remove the pen by pulling it upwards .

How to Load or Unload Cartridges?

What are Cricut Cartridges? Cricut cartridges are a library of images that users can buy to use in creating their projects on their Cricut machine. Usually, these cartridges collect images focusing on a season (e. g Christmas or Easter), characters, or concept. A certain common trait links all the content of a cartridge together.

The Cartridges are physical devices that you plug into your Cricut Explore Air. You plug the cartridge into the cartridge port.

Within Cricut Access there are lots of "Cricut cartridges". These cartridges are not physical cartridges; they are digital libraries just like the physical cartridges. Once you purchase a cartridge, you can use it even without a subscription to Cricut Access. You can use Cartridges from your older machine on your Cricut Explore Air. Once linked to your account, you can have access to the content of the cartridge without even the physical unit.

With Cricut Access there is little need to get physical cartridges .

Cricut Explorer comes with the feature of using cartridges. To use a cartridge first, you need to open up Design Space using our Cricut account. Open up the green account button and click on the link cartridge option. A new page will open, which is the link cartridge window. Now turn on the Cricut Explorer and put the cartridge in the cartridge slot. The cartridge label should be facing forward, and it should be fully set. When the software air recognizes the cartridge in the device, then click 'link cartridge' at the lower right corner of the screen.

The screen will confirm whether the cartridge has been linked or not. Now the cartridge can be safely removed. To access the cartridges files, first, you should open Design Space with your Cricut ID. Then click on the ownership icon and select purchased. Now find the cartridge that you are looking for. To insert the items in your cartridge onto a design, on the Design Space window, click on insert and search for the cartridge by name or click on the cartridge icon .

How to Load or Unload a Debossing Tool?

Debossing tool, also called a debossing tip, is used to press on the materials giving it an everlasting imprint. Instead of a solid end, it has a rollerball which allows the color to slide onto the material rather than dragging on. This feature gives sharp images and opens up new possibilities. It is used in the Cricut Maker. It goes into the Quickswap housing and like any other blade into clamp B.

Linking Cartridges with the Cricut Explore Air

While you cannot use your machine offline, your cartridges will work fine. Here is how to link your cartridge with the Cricut Explore Air.

Using your browser, visit www.cricut.com/design and sign into your account .

After logging in, click on the account button (it is green in color).

Click on "Cartridge Linking" from the drop-down menu.

Fix the cartridge firmly in the cartridge port. Ensure the machine is switched on and connected to the PC.

The cartridge if detected will trigger an alert prompting you to link the cartridge to your account.

Click "Link Cartridge"

Pairing the Cricut machine through Bluetooth to the Computer

To get your Cricut Explore Air 2 paired with your computer or mobile device, you are required to take the following steps: - Make sure your Wireless Bluetooth Adapter is in place and working.

- Have the Cricut Explore Air 2 turned on, and it should be at most 15 feet from your PC.

- Check to be sure your computer is Bluetooth enabled by taking the following sub-steps on your computer.

❖ Go to the "Start button" and right-click on it.

❖ Select the "Device Manager. "

❖ If you have the Bluetooth listed in the device manager, definitely it is Bluetooth enabled; otherwise, you will have to get a USB device referred to as Bluetooth Dongle to get your computer interacting with other Bluetooth devices.

- You can now close your Device manager once you have confirmed it is Bluetooth enabled.

- Go to the "Start menu."

- Select "Settings."

- Go to the "Devices" option and open it.

- Make sure the Bluetooth is active and select "Include Bluetooth or another device.

- Click on "Bluetooth," you can then grab a cup of coffee while your PC searches for and pairs with the Cricut Machine.

- Select the Cricut machine once it appears on the list.

- In a case where you are prompted to input in a PIN, type in 0000 and click on "Connect."

- Once you select the Connect option, your Cricut Explore Air 2 machine will now be paired to your computer .

NOTE: THE CRICUT EXPLORE AIR 2 MACHINE MIGHT SHOW UP AS AN Audio on the Bluetooth list. If this happens, its okay, and you can go ahead with pairing.

In a situation where you have multiple Cricut machines, make use of the device code in identifying which one you like to pair. The device code can be found on the serial number tag at the bottom of the machine.

Unpairing or removing the Bluetooth device

The removal or unpairing of your Bluetooth device from the Cricut Explore Air 2 varies based on the version of the operating system in use. You are required to take the following steps in the process of unpairing or removing the Bluetooth device: - Go to the Start menu - Select Settings - Select the Devices option - Choose the device you want to remove and click on the "Remove device."

- You will be prompted to confirm your action .

Resetting the Cricut Explore Air 2 Machine

When some issues arise with your machine, there might be a need to perform a hard reset for such a problem to be resolved. In performing the hard reset, you are required to take the following steps: - Turn off the Cricut Explore Air 2 machine.

- Simultaneously hold down the Magnifying glass, pause as well as the power buttons.

- Hold the three buttons down simultaneously until the machine displays a rainbow screen, and you can release the buttons afterward.

- Promptly follow the on-screen instructions that follow.

- Get the process repeated one more time.

How to Cut Heavyweight and Lightweight Materials

Before delving into this project, I would like to explain a few important tips for this project that will help you accomplish the task accurately. Go over them as much as you can to fully understand each of these tips. It will definitely help you .

Do not eject the mat when you pause the machine to clean or replace a blunt rotary blade. If you remove the mat, it will be difficult to get the correct alignment of the cut and finish your project with accuracy. So, what you can do is pause the machine, remove the rotary blade, clean or replace the rotary blade, put it back in and hit the Cricut button to continue. You will have to do all these without ejecting the mat because if you do eject the mat, you terminate your project and will start all over.

Before you unload your material from the machine, make sure that you check your project and that the cut has been done all the way. If the cut is not all the way, you can restart the cut all over as long as you did not eject or move the mat.

The Design space will also be notifying you of the progress of the cut: how many passes to complete your project, and the amount of time remaining to finish your project. This is amazing as it will help you get the progress of your work any time you check on it. That is, in case, you need to carry out other pressing task at hand .

The materials required for this project includes Cricut machine (Maker or Expression), 3" x 24" Bass wood, rotary blade, and painter's tape.

The first thing, as usual, is to design your text to be cut on Cricut Design space. In case you don't know how to do that, please go to the sections How to Design with Cricut Machine and How to Edit Text in Cricut Design Space.

There is no room for assumptions here because it will save you time and money too. But if you already know that and you have your design ready, it is time to go the task at hand.

1. You have the design in your Cricut design space, so click Continue.

Select the type of material by clicking on Browse All Materials.

Type in Bass wood in the materials and choose the type of Bass wood, preferably 1/16 Basswood.

Click Done. Ensure that you follow the instructions on the cutting window by moving the star wheel to the right of the machine. I believe that you still remember why this is important? Then, the materials should be secured to the Strong Grip mat using tape. Of course, the material should not be more 11" wide.

Insert the rotary blade to the accessory clamp. By the way, the machine will give a warning if the blade is not inserted.

Now, you load the mat into the machine by pressing on the Load/Unload button.

The machine will start cutting when you press the flashing Cricut button. It will make an entire pass of the image the machine is going to cut before cutting the full image. Of course, this will take time because of the thickness of the cut. Therefore, you can do other pressing task at hand.

Unload the mat by pressing the Load/Unload button which will be blinking when the task is complete.

Remove the tape and your material from the mat.

Use the weeding tool to remove your design from the whole material gently.

Working on this project would have stirred your creative mind on many ideas you can accomplish following this approach.

CHAPTER 3: CRICUT DESIGN SPACE SOFTWARE FOR CRICUT EXPLORE AIR 2

How to Upload Images with A Cricut Explore Air 2?

❧❦❧

Uploading your images to Design Space is a walk in the park once you get a grip on the basic concepts. As stated earlier, there are two significant categories of image files that can be uploaded to the Design Space.

Vector Images; .dxf and .svg files. They are uploaded in more than one layer in such a way that you can edit varying independent parts in the platform.

Basic Images; .png, .jp, .gif and .bmp are uploaded in the form of a single-layered image. This implies that what you see in the preview of the image before printing and cutting is exactly what you will get after the whole process is completed .

After your image is ready, which you might have bought on the Cricut platform or designed yourself, the time is now here to upload it. The next logical step to take is to open the Design Space.

Tap on the 'Browse Files" tab and search for the relevant file from your PC.

If the file is a vector image, a preview will come up after the upload is complete. At this point, you can rename the image and save it from this point.

On the other hand, if the file is a basic image, you can carry out any of the following functions: - Select the type of vision; this serves to determine the complexity of the picture. If the image been uploaded does not contain too much information, you can pick the Simple Image option, and if the details in the image are much, you can select the Moderately or Complex Image Options.

- Tap on the Continue icon.

- Select and Erase; here, you can carry out the editing process on your basic image. This involves erasing and cropping out the unneeded parts by making use of the available tools .

When you are satisfied with the result, tap on the continue button.

- Name and Tag; in this section, you can give your image a name and also decide if it will be a cut image or a print and cut image.

- Save - You will then be taken back to the upload image screen.

The image is now prepared and ready to be cut or printed.

Adding Fonts

A lot of folks have the misconceptions that they need to add fonts to Design Space. The truth here is that you do not need to do that. To get your desired fonts, you will have to download them to your PC and then install it. The downloaded fonts will only be available on the system to which you downloaded and installed it on and not on any other system in which you log into your Design Space account on.

Go with the following steps to download and install fonts to the Design Space on your PC

Get a site where you can download the fonts from. Here are some of the websites that you can make use of; esty.com, fornsquirrel.com, fontspace.com, creativemarket.com, datfont.com. Note that some of the fonts are free, while others are not. If your finished product is going to be sold, you should obtain the license or get commercially free fonts. On any of the sites that you choose to get your font from, you can browse through the catalogue available there to pick the one that best suits your current project. Click on download when you have decided on the font you want to go with. It will download straight to your PC.

Search for the downloaded file on your PC, or better still, go straight to the Downloads Folder, it will most likely be there. The data comes in a zipped folder, unzip it (right-click on your mouse or the touchpad, and select the undo option) to get access to the fonts.

When you are in the file, tap twice in quick succession on the .ttf file. A prompt will come up initiating the installation of the fonts, tap on confirm to begin the process.

Open your Design Space and open a new page, and from there, click on the text tool. Enter a sentence or a word and then move onto the font selection option. You can tap on the system option to have a look at all the fonts that are installed on your PC or simply enter the name of the font that you want .

Despite the vast library of custom images, the Cricut Design Space has, there are files that you may want to cut yourself that may not be available in the system. Since Cricut Design Space supports DIY designs, you can design your own files and upload them to the Design Space for cutting. You can either use Adobe Illustrator or Photoshop to create your own designs.

To upload and use images

Open the Cricut Design Space environment and click, "Upload Image" from the left-hand menu.

Browse through the list of uploaded files and select the image.

Select, "Insert Image".

Select from the type of images Cricut Design Space will ask you.

Another tab will open, select the part of the image you want to cut and the one you do not want to.

Choose whether your image is a regular image or a print-then-cut image.

The file will appear in your work area on the screen. Sometimes, the imported data do not come at the correct dimensions, so you would have to edit. The "edit" menu is on the right of the screen.

Select, "Go" in the top right of the screen and cut your design .

Making a Vinyl Sticker

First of all, you need to have an idea of the vinyl sticker that you want. Get ideas online or from forums. Once you have gotten the picture, make a sketch if it to see how the sticker would look. After you have done this, follow the steps below;

Use an image editing software like Photoshop or Illustrator. Design to your taste and save. Make sure you know the folder it is saved to.

Now, open your Design Space.

Click "New Project".

Scroll to the bottom left-hand side and click "Upload".

Drag and drop the design you created with your photo editing app.

Select your image type. If you want to keep your design simple, select simple.

Select which area of the image that is not part of it.

Before you forge ahead, select the image as cut to have a preview. You can go back if there is a need for adjustments.

Select "Cut".

Weed excess vinyl.

Use a transfer tape on top of the vinyl. This will make the vinyl stay in position.

Go over the tape and ensure all the bibles are nowhere to be found.

Peel away the transfer tape and you have your vinyl sticker.

Best Tools and Software's for Cricut Machine Explore Air 2

Cutting Mat

The Cutting Mat gives a platform on how the materials are going to be laid into the Cricut Machine.

The cutting mat is designed to be sticky on one of the sides to securely hold the material in place during the cutting, scoring, or inking process.

The cutting mat is made up of three types, with each of them used for different kinds of materials. So, the kind of cutting mat you choose to use solely depends on the materials you are working with.

Here are the three types of Cutting mats as well as the materials that work with each of them:

- Standard Grip (the one in green color)
- Window clings
- Vinyl
- Regular with Embossed cardstock
- Heat transfer (Iron-on) with regular vinyl
- Firm Grip (the one in purple color)

- Magnetic material
- Foam
- Wood as well as Balsa
- Posterboard
- Backed fabric
- Corrugated Cardboard
- Leather with Suede
- Chipboard
- Light grip (blue color)
- Light cardstock
- Construction paper
- Printer with scrapbook paper
- Vellum

Cutting Mat Covers

The plastic shield is used for covering the cutting mat when purchased. The plastic shield can be pulled off and placed back quickly.

You are always advised to keep and place back the cover of the mat after you are done ever to keep the cloth clean and helps maintain the stickiness.

It is important to always wipe over your cutting mat with some baby wipes. In cleaning your cutting mat, the nonalcoholic baby wipes are recommended to keep your cutting mat from building up with vinyl and cardstock residue after cutting processes.

It also keeps it clean from specks of dust and lint that may be floating about.

Tool Cup

The tool cup is the part that holds scissors, pens, and other Cricut tools in use. The pen is used by getting the accessory clamp A opened and dropping in the pen down into it, after which the clamp is then closed .

Accessory Storage Compartments Apart from the Tool Cup, the

Cricut Explore Air 2 machine is made up of two compartments which are also used in holding tools, these are: - Smaller Compartment - Larger Compartment

The smaller compartment is positioned at the left for holding additional blade housings, the accessory adapter as well as the blades. The lower chamber is made up of a magnetic strip for securely keeping the replacement blades and prevents it from rolling.

The larger compartment is used to store more extended tools and pens.

Accessory Clamp A

The accessory clamp A comes preinstalled as the accessory adapter, and the pen for drawing instead for having to cut can be inserted through this part. It also helps in holding the scoring blades .

The Cricut Scoring Stylus

The Cricut Scoring Stylus is an essential tool, especially for your card projects. So on purchase, it is necessary to check to make sure this tool comes with the Cricut machine.

They are available for free when you purchase the Cricut machine.

Blade Clamp A

Cricut Explore Air Machine has the Blade clamp A already preinstalled in them. The replacement or the removal of bits of vinyl can also be done here.

Smart Set dial

The Cricut Explore Air machine, through its fast mode of operation, enables the user to turn and indicate which material is to be cut with the twice fast style with the use of the Smart Set dial. All you need to do is to rotate the Smart Set dial and choose the material you will be cutting.

Removing and Replacing the Accessory and the Blade clamps of the Cricut Explore Air Machine To remove the accessory clamp or blade, pull open the lever, after which you will then get the metal housing pulled out.

The blade is positioned seated inside; having a tiny plunger on the top, pressing this down will reveal the edge which is held out magnetically.

To get the blade replaced, if the need arises, all you have to do is to get the edge pulled out and drop the new knife in.

Standard Grip Cutting Mat:

The cutting mat is sticky in nature. It is made sticky so that it holds the material being cut in place as it is being cut. Before any operations are carried out, the material to be cut or written on is placed on the Cutting Mat. The mat serves as the work surface for the machine.

Blade and Housing:

This comes preinstalled in the machine. The blade and its housing are attached to one of the two tool holders. You can get other blades and blade holders to cut unique material s

Cricut Cardstock:

In the box, you have some cardstock. This lets you hit the ground running and begin your first project. The cardstock comes in different colors and textures. You could purchase extra material if the cardstock provided in the box proves to be inadequate.

Pen and Accessory Adapter:

The adapter is preinstalled on the second tool holder. It is on this tool holder that the pen or any other accessory is affixed. The adapter holds whatever accessory you wish to use on the secondary tool holder. To use a pen with it, you simply drop a pen into it.

Power Cord:

The Cricut Explore Air 2 runs on electricity. The power cord connects the machine to a power outlet.

USB Cord:

The USB cord connects the device to the computer. It is vital to compare the Cricut Explore Air 2 to the computer with the USB cord when connecting for the first time. This lets the necessary drivers be installed in the networks. After the essential drivers get installed, subsequent connections can be made wirelessly.

Mat Guides:

The Mat Guides are found on the sides of the tray. They keep the Cutting Mat firmly in place and prevent it from moving as the material upon it is being cut. This helps achieve exact and intricate cuts.

Rollers:

The rollers work to push the material being operated under the tool holders so that they can be worked on. The Cutting Mat is placed on the rollers and they roll back and forth to push the cutting mat back and forth. This was the tool holder can reach all parts of the material being worked on to give an exact cut.

How to Cut Vinyl from A Cricut Machine?

First, place the Vinyl liner side down onto the Standard grip mat. Then place it inside the machine after selecting the design. Push the go button to start .

For a smooth placement of the vinyl, you should use vinyl transfer tape. Transfer tape is a kind of pre-mask that transfer vinyl graphics to a substrate after being cut and weeded.

After cutting is done, remove the negatives of the image by a weeder or a tweezer, only leaving the wanted design on the mat. Now remove the Transfer Tape liner. Carefully with the sticky side down, place it on the mat with the design. Gently press to remove any air bubbles.

Whatever surface you want the design on, it should be clean and dry. Carefully place the vinyl on the surface and gently press it down. Remove the tap by peeling it off at a 45-degree angle. If it is difficult, burnish it by using a scrapper.

How to Cut Basswood by Cricut?

For cutting a word, make sure that it is not thicker than 11 mm. Use a strong grip mat for its cutting. Handle the wood carefully as the wood can be more fragile and easier to break. Use a craft knife and a ruler for this project. Clean the wood or use compressed air to remove all the dust. Mirror the images on Design Space. Brayer can be used to provide adhesion to the mat. Remove the white wheelers to the side of the machine. Check that the wood is not under the rollers; otherwise, it can cause damage. Make sure the design stays inside the edges of the wood — test before cutting the project.

How to design with Cricut machine

I know that you have lot of ideas stuck in your brain and looking for a way to express them. What you need to do is set up your Cricut Explore Air machine, set up the Design Space, and start expressing those ideas immediately.

WORKING WITH FONTS IN THE DESIGN SPACE

One of the unique features of the Cricut Design Space is the ability to brand your project with distinct fonts and text. Most project with Cricut machines start with the Design Space and you know what? There is more to it than meet the eye. Let me start with fonts in the Design Space .

HOW TO ADD TEXT TO CRICUT DESIGN SPACE

For users of Windows, navigate to the left-hand side of the Canvas and select the Text tool. For iOS or Android user, the Text tool is at the bottom-left of the screen.

Select the font size and the font type you wish to use and then type your text in the text box. Do not freak out when you did not choose the font parameters before typing the text, with Cricut Design Space, you can type the text before selecting the font on Windows/Mac computer.

Click or tap on any space outside the text box to close it.

HOW TO EDIT TEXT IN CRICUT DESIGN SPACE

To edit the text is super simple. Double click on the text to show available options. Select the action you wish from the list of the options displayed including font style, type, size, letter and line spacing.

HOW TO EDIT FONTS

Select the text you wish to edit on the Canvas or you can insert text from design panel, or select a text layer from the Layers Panel.

When the Text Edit Bar pops up, you can start changing the font using the available options. These options include Font, Font DropDown, Font Filter, Style, Font Size, Line Space, Alignment, and more.

A simple way to write font using Cricut pen with Cricut Explore Air machine is to change the line type of your text from 'Cut' to 'Write'. Next is to choose the font type you wish to use and select the "Writing style" of your choice. Note that the fonts used in the Writing style is similar to the text written by hand but the Cricut machine will write it as if it is tracing the outside of the letters. I believe you know how to use fonts now and what the final form of the fonts will look like. Now, I want to discuss the different types of fonts.

System Fonts

System fonts refer to fonts installed on your computer or mobile device. Every time you sign in, the Cricut Design Space will automatically access your system fonts and allow you to use them for free in the Design Space projects.

Some system fonts have design components that are not compatible with Cricut Design space because they were not designed by Cricut. Do not be surprise when you encounter failure to import them into the Design Space, or they behave unusual while using them in the Design Space. Use the instructions on the font site or app when downloading fonts to your device or computer .

Finding the current firmware version
on my machine

It is recommended to have the updated version of the firmware of your device for optimal effective use. This part of the book helps with the latest firmware version that is available for all the Cricut machines.

Finding the current firmware version of the Cricut Explore machines - Make sure you have your Cricut Explore machine connected and powered on.

- Sign in to the Cricut Design Space.

- Go to the upper left corner of the Design space and select the account menu.

- Select the "Update Firmware"

- You will be prompted with a pop-window, select your machine out of the dropdown list and give the software a few moments to detect your machine.

- You will receive a message letting you know if your firmware is up to date or not once your machine has been detected. If your machine is not up to date, you will be notified of any available updates .

. . .

<u>HERE IS THE LIST OF THE LATEST FIRMWARE VERSIONS:</u>

Cricut Explore: 1.091

Cricut Explore Air: 3.091

Cricut Explore Air 2: 5.120

Cricut Explore one: 2.095

Cricut Maker: 4.175

IT IS TO BE NOTED THAT THE CRICUT EXPLORE AIR OR CRICUT Maker firmware can also be checked making use of the Design Space on the computer.

Finding the current version of Design Space

To help get the best result with the use of your Cricut Explore Air, it is recommended that you make use of your latest software version. As updates are being released, this actual version changes. To find the current version of the Design Space, you are required to take the following steps: - Go to the taskbar and click on the arrow to display the hidden icons.

- Place your mouse and hover on the Cricut Design space icon .

- Once you hover on the Cricut Design Space, the plugin version should come up.

The Fast Mode of the Cricut Explore
Air machine and how it is used

The Cricut Explore Air 2 machine is designed to work in the fast mode, which allows the machine to cut and write up to two times faster than we have in the previous Cricut Explore models. The fast mode is also employed in the Cricut Makers machines as well.

The Fast mode features are made available with the Iron-on, Vinyl, and Cardstock material settings, which are set to Vinyl to Cardstock+ on the Smart Set dial available on the Explore machine.

To make use of the Fast Mode feature of the Cricut Explore Air machine, here are the basic instructions that you will need to follow: - When all is set for writing and cutting your project, simply go to the Cut screen.

- The Fast Mode option will be made available if you have chosen the right material for the mode.

- Toggle the switch to the "ON" position by clicking or tapping the switch to get the Fast Mode activated. It is to be noted that the Cricut Explore Air 2 machines tend to make a louder noise while making use of the fast mode features; this is normal.

Cleaning and Care

Cleaning your Cricut machine involves basically caring for your mat. All other cleanings will have to do with maintenance of your machine.

There are different ways of cleaning Cricut mat based on their types:

FOR FABRICGRIP CRICUT MAT:

Do not use scrapper tool to remove bits of fabric on the Cricut mat unlike other Cricut mats

The oils on your finger can reduce the adhesive on the mat's surface, therefore, avoid touching of the surface with your fingers.

Use only Cricut spatula, tweezers or StronGrip transfer tape to clean this mat.

Cleaning agents including soap and water should not be used on this mat

FOR OTHER MATS:

Use the tool called scrapper to clear all the leftovers from your Cricut mat

For smaller leftover bits difficult to remove, use a sticky lint roller and roll it over your Cricut mat to remove them.

Wash your Cricut mat with any gentle detergent and water then leave to dry.

Use nonalcoholic cleaning wipe to clan the surface of your Cricut mat.

Cutting Blade

Every single blade you use might get up to fifteen thousand individual cuts before it needs to be replaced. To prolong this number of individual cuts, place the aluminum foil onto the cutting mat and cut out a few designs. This process keeps the blade extra sharp and lengthens the life of the blade. This number of cuts can be greatly based on the types of materials cut by the blade. If you are doing many projects in which thick materials need to be cut the blade will deteriorate quickly; the blade can also deteriorate quickly if you are cutting many materials on high pressure. A good way to know if your blade needs to be replaced is if your cuts' quality starts to decrease greatly. If this happens it's best to replace the cutting blade. When replacing the blade, it is always best to get blades that are Cricut brand. Generic blades are often not the best quality and will cause you to replace your cutting blade constantly. To install the new blade once you've ordered the correct one, you need first to unplug your Cricut Cutter machine. Always unplug the machine before installing anything in your Cricut cutter. Next, you must remove the old, dull cutting blade from your Cricut Cutter machine. The process of how to do this has been mentioned numerous times in this book and the last chapter. Once the cutting blade assembly has been separated it is now time to eject the blade. Find the small silver button above the adjustment knob and press the button down; this will eject the cutting blade. Be very careful when doing this as the blade is extremely sharp and can easily cut through the skin. Keep all blades away from children and pets. To put in the new blade, insert the blade on the end of the blade assembly opposite of the blade release button. The blade will then be pulled up into the assembly. Place the assembly back into the machine by reversing the process previously written about in the last chapter.

GETTING THE CRICUT CUTTING MAT CLEANED

It is important to always wipe over your cutting mat with some baby wipes. In cleaning your cutting mat, the non-alcoholic baby wipes are recommended to keep your cutting mat from building up with vinyl and cardstock residue after cutting processes.

It also keeps it clean from specks of dust and lint that may be floating about.

The Cutting mat in addition to the cutting blade needs to be taken care of. One cutting mat can have a life of anywhere from twenty-five to forty cuts. The cutting mat's experience can vary from this amount depending on the pressure and speed at which the cuts have been made and the type of materials that have been cut on the mat. To prolong the life of your cutting mat, remove any debris from the mat after a cut and always avoid scraping the mat.

If you scrape the mat, it can push any debris further into the mat. After each craft, it is best to run lukewarm water over the mat and dab it dry with a towel afterward. When a material can not adhere to the cutting mat any longer, it is time to replace it finally. It is recommended to get many cutting mats and rotate between them to prolong all the cutting mats. This extends the mats' life because one cutting mat will not be cut on for many, many projects in a small amount of time. It is also recommended that you keep all of your cutting mats and all of your cartridges and blades in a very organized manner. Throwing the haphazardly components can destroy and deteriorate them so it is best to keep them in a very organized fashion. A benefit of keeping your Cricut Cutter components organized is that you won't lose or damage the very expensive items necessary for several projects.

. . .

CRICUT MACHINE

The final thing to keep clean is the actual Cricut Cutter machine. The machine needs to be wiped down with a damp cloth. Only wipe down the external panels of the machine and with the machine unplugged. Always wipe down the machine with a dry cloth after cleaning the outside of the machine. Never clean the Cricut Cutter machine with abrasive cleaners such as acetone, benzene, and all other alcohol-based cleaners. Abrasive cleaning tools should never be used on the Cricut Cutter machine either. Also, never submerge any machine component or the Cricut Cutter machine into the water as it can damage the device.

Always keep the Cricut Cutter machine away from all foods, liquids, pets, and children. Keep the Cricut Cutter machine in a very dry and dust free environment. Finally, do not put the Cricut Cutter machine in excessive heat, excessive cold, sunlight, or any area where the plastic or any other components on the Cricut Cutter machine can melt.

Using or creating custom material settings

The Cricut Explore Air machines are used for cutting different kinds of materials. It is designed with pre-programmed settings on the design space to create flexibility when working on projects using various materials. Apart from these pre-programmed settings, you can create your own as well.

Making use of Custom material settings - Get signed into the Design Space and create a project .

- Turn on your Cricut Explore machine.

- Have your Cricut Explore machine connected to your computer.

- Go to the Project Preview screen and ensure that the Smart Set Dial is appropriately locked to Custom.

- Click on "Browse All Materials."

You can simply search for the material by name or scrolling to browse the list. Note that all the materials having the Cricut logo next to them are the Cricut branded materials.

. . .

How to create a new Custom material

This becomes handy in a situation where your choice of material is not available on the materials list. When this happens, you can simply try the settings with the closest match to your material or build a new setting.

It is important to note that new Custom materials cannot be added to the Cricut Design space when using the Android device. Still, any materials that are added from the Computer, iPhone, or iPad will be made available on the Android app.

To create a new material setting, you are required to take the following steps below: - Go to the menu and select the "Manage Custom Materials" or select the "Materials Settings" located at the bottom of the page when browsing materials for projects to gain access to the Custom Materials screen.

- Select the "Add New Material" by scrolling down to the bottom of the list.

- Have the name of the material indicated.

- Click on the "Save" option.

- After saving the material, you will have the chance to make necessary adjustments with the use of the following: ❖ Multi-cut: This helps in directing the machine to cut multiple times in the same image, and it is usually used for thick materials.

❖ Cut pressure: This adjusts the slider or using the +/- buttons.

❖ Blade type: You can select from the deep-point blade or high-grade Fine-Point blade for the Design Space to prompt accordingly.

❖ Select "Save" to get your new custom material saved after configuration.

❖ Close the materials screen with the "X" sign that will be found at the top-right corner.

After this, your new material will be found in the materials list and can be found using the search option. It is to be noted that the star can be used in adding the material to your favorite .

Cut Vinyl with A Cricut Machine

There are different types of vinyl that you can use.

Oracal 651, I would recommend using it for PERMANENT works as the strong adhesive might compromise your surface and leave a lot of residue. It is perfect for outdoors works because it is water resistant. But you can generally choose Oracal 651 for your indoor creation that you know you will make a heavy use with, like mugs, plates, bowls. But this might not be working for everyone, so I recommend you first give a try in one mug or two.

Oracal 631 is generally used for wall decals and other internal works and it is appreciated because it can last a little while but can't stand up to heavy applications. So, it is NOT PERMANENT. However, you can create infinite things with it, like phone cases, interior decorations, stencils, etc...

HEAT TRANSFER VINYL (MORE KNOWN AS HTV)

This is a common and easy to apply method, also for who is starting from scratch. After cutting the vinyl piece, you use your iron to apply the vinyl to a fabric surface. It holds up through the washing machine and looks very professional. You can customize your favorite clothing. As you are reading in this guide, this method is also known as T-Shirt Vinyl or Iron-on Vinyl. There is a variety of brands, but the most often recommended is Scissor Easy Weed. Easy to use, it comes in various styles and colors and it holds up through the washing machine, it looks perfect. It is ideal for: Socks, T-shirts, and Stuffed animals, Canvas tote bags, Costumes, anything with fabric

PRINTABLE VINYL

Printable Vinyl comes both in Heat Transfer and Adhesive types. All you need to have with this particular material is a normal inkjet printer. The design can be printed out on your vinyl.

Using Snap Mat cutting multiple Colors

Take pieces of vinyl of different colors, cut and put them all on your Cricut Mat, and make it easier to take a picture of it, I suggest laying your mat on the floor. Then from your Cricut App, click categories, then Projects in the Cloud, then select the project you will cut and click customize, then replace and then Make it .

Next click on Snap Mat and you can place the camera over the floor on your Mat and wait for the box to turn green, hold it for a few seconds and take the picture.

Once the picture popped up, select use, and then select continue. You can start your creation with multiple colors in one mat. You can create images and text and swipe from one color to another.

Cricut Scrapbooking

Scrapbooking is the most recent crafty phenomenon. With the introduction of digital electronic cameras, traditional picture albums have gone by the wayside and better method to keep essential photos and the memories attached. There are many tools for avid scrapbookers from various papers, stickers, shapes and scissors; would it not be fantastic to have all these products in one main place and at the touch of a button? Cricut Expression is the answer. This individual electronic cutter enables you to produce some of the most individualized and beautiful shapes to include flare to even you're the majority of papercraft standards .

Those concerned that a maker might waste paper by not making use of all the areas available, do not worry. The Cricut has been created not only to develop terrific shapes and font styles, however it will do it in such as the manner in it will make the most of the user of the paper, which will help keep the amount of waste to a minimum.

How do you desire to get your words onto your page?

The simplest is to find a writing design you like and practice up until you are more than happy with it. Otherwise it's a trip to your regional scrapbook shop to spend your robust generated income on alphabets - again!

So ... having filled the dishwasher, the cleaning machine and the drier, got the kids to school, made appointments for the hair and the dental professional dresser for everyone, went to the PTA meeting and got the groceries for dinner, you just have time between your lunch date with hubby and gathering the dry cleansing to run to the scrapbook store before it's time to gather the kids from school, offer them a snack, prepare supper so it's prepared when you all get back from soccer practice, then house once again to consume dinner, aid with research, get the kids to bed, and go over some household issues with hubby before you hit the sack yourself ... By the method, when do you have time to scrapbook?

Anyway, when you do make it to the scrapbook store what you will discover there? You need to create humungous choices:

• Alphabet Sticker Labels Rub-Ons

- Die Cuts Stamps
- Word and Expression Decorations

ANY OF THESE COULD MAKE FANTASTIC TITLES, JOURNALING AND beliefs on your designs. Let's have a look at some of them;

ALPHABET STICKER LABELS

The disadvantage is they never seem to come with adequate letters, and you can only make a couple of words in the same style. Nevertheless, you can utilize the remaining letters as 'drop capitals' at the beginning of paragraphs in your design.

You can get off with a range of different styles in this method by adding some layouts, that will allow you to mix and match different designs within the title or bullets. It's enjoyable to include casual style characters in the middle of your journaling, too.

Rubon

These were called transfers when I was a child, and only came as letters. They now come as individual letters or words and expressions in black or various colors, and numerous gorgeous designs, too.

As the name recommends, you merely rub them onto your page with the little stick offered. If you lose the stick.), (You can utilize a bone folder or a coin It's an excellent concept to cut around the words you desire to use and position them thoroughly or you may find stray pieces from the word next door that you hadn't meant to transfer.

Rub-on looks good and provides a professional finish.

Alphabet stamps

These are an excellent buy as you can prevent the 'never-have-all-the-letters-I-need' syndrome that occurs with other media - and they are re-useable !

If you choose for clear stamps, it's simple to stamp words with duplicate letters. Simply line up the letters on a clear acrylic block to form your word, leaving the correct size area for the replicate letters which you add on a 2nd pass.

To conserve the right space, put another stamp in the place where the replicate letter will go, and when you've completed the word remove it and you're entrusted to an area where you mark the missing letter later on. You can stamp the letters accurately since you can see where you are stamping. After use, simply wipe clean, change on the sheet and they're prepared for next time!

Electronic and mechanical systems

The numerous cutting machine systems have some terrific alphabets, but, if you are brand-new to scrapbooking they can seem an expensive way to develop your titles. Suppose you believe you will also use some of the many other shapes readily available. In that case, the results are outstanding and well worth the cost. You will get exceptional usage out of these mainly if you make your own greetings cards, too.

Before you make the trip to your regional scrapbooking store consider utilizing your computer system. You currently have a variety of font styles on it and there are much more available to download devoid of the web.

Your computer is one of the most flexible ways to develop a title or journaling. With the massive selection of typefaces available you will discover one that fits your layout design, but much more beneficial is the versatility when it comes to size. You can have the font as large as you desire for a title, or little sufficient to get all your journaling on a tag.

You will conserve a lot of money with the aid of your computer system.

. . .

How do you get titles from your computer to your design?

It's fast and effortless to do.

Select a font style and size it appropriately for your task.

Type your words, and then print using the reverse image setting on your printer alternatives .

Transfer to the incorrect side of your picked pattern or color paper or cardstock,

Cut out and stay with your scrapbook job or card.

If you don't have, or can't find the reverse image setting, then: thoroughly trace around your words - a lightbox will help you here - on the ideal side of the paper, cut out inside your lines.

It's great to have so many ranges of alphabets for our designs. However, do attempt to avoid using one design too typically, as it will be monotonous to make and to view an album filled with the very same styles.

Now you see how simple it is to make excellent titles and journaling, there's nothing stopping you. Have a good time creating your memories - and might you have time to preserve them on lovely scrapbook page designs.

CHAPTER 4: SOLVING THE MOST COMMON PROBLEM WHEN USING CRICUT EXPLORE AIR 2

Helpful Troubleshooting Techniques

Problems with printing images

The Explore machine will work with various printers, but some printers will jam when using card stock. The best option is to use a printer that feeds the card stock from the rear. The less turns the card stock makes in the printer the less chance of it jamming.

Play it safe and don't use a laser printer for vinyl or sticky material. The heat of the printer will melt the material and could damage the printer.

Design Space has a printable area that is 6.75 by 9.25. This is a lot bigger than past versions.

When you're working with an image, you're going to print select a square from the Shapes tool and place it behind your image. Make the size of the square 6.75 and 9.25. Then you can see while you're working with you image whether or not it is within the printable area. Make the square a light color so you can see it separate from your image.

You can put more than one image in the box. Attach the images so you can move them all at one time. Delete the box before printing.

It's easier than ever to create custom designs for multiple uses by changing their Line type instead of redesigning the whole project.

Pens

When you're inserting a pen into your machine, place a piece of scrap paper under the pen. This keeps the pen from marking up your material or your machine when you click it into the clamp.

There are several ways to breathe new life into dried markers sometimes just soaking the tip will work or refilling the pen with 90% alcohol.

Besides the homemade universal pen adapter I mentioned, the tube shaped pencil grips fit some markers making them compatible with the Explore .

Problems with cutting images

Before unloading the mat try to determine if the material has been cut to satisfaction. If not manually hit the cut button on the Explore and cut it again several times.

Use the Custom Material Settings in Design Space to increase or decrease the pressure, add multiple cuts, choose an intricate cut setting, or change materials. Within each category there are several listings for different kinds of paper or card stock for example. Just try selecting another type and see if that helps.

Create your own custom settings for any material by selecting Manage Custom Materials from the main menu. Then just click Add New Material and enter the information.

Some intricate designs won't cut well in Fast Mode so just cut it regularly. Make sure the blade and mat are clean.

If your images are not cutting correctly be sure and wipe the mat and scrape off any access material left from previous projects. If the mat is severely scored or gouged replace it .

Try switching to another mat such as the stickier blue mat. If the mat isn't sticky enough the material can slip and won't cut properly. Or tape the paper to the mat.

Then carefully clean the blade. If there is still a problem, it might be time to replace the blade. Using the new German Carbide blade is your best option for optimal cutting. Believe it or not there can be a slight difference in the cutting edge between one new blade and another.

Make sure the blade fits tightly in the housing. Regularly clean out the blade housing of fibers that accumulate and interfere with the cutting process. Blow into the housing or use a straightened paperclip and carefully loosen and stuck material.

Since the deep cutting blade angle is different, try using it on regular material when experiencing problems.

If you get a message saying image is too large you simply need to resize it to make it smaller. Some people think that since the mat is 12 x 12 they can use 12 x 12 images. But there is a little space left for margins, so the largest image size is 11.5 x 11.5. You can purchase a 12 x 24 mat to make larger cuts of 11.5 x 23.5 .

If all else fails, try a different material. Some users find that certain brands of paper or card stock work better than others.

Mats

If your mat is too sticky when it's new place a white T-shirt on it and press lightly or just pat it with your hands. This will reduce some of the stickiness.

When using a brayer and thin paper don't apply a lot of pressure on the mat. This makes it hard to remove without ripping the paper.

Always clean your mat after each use. Use a scraper to remove small bits of lint or paper that have been left behind. These small scraps will cause problems with future projects.

You can wipe the mat with a damp cloth. Then replace the plastic cover between uses to prevent dust and dirt from sticking to the mat.

When the mat has lost its stickiness; tape the material to the mat around the edges or wash it with a little soap and water, rinse, let dry and it's good to go .

Have you seen those food grade flexible cutting mats or boards? Some users are turning them into Cricut mats. Look for the thin plastic ones that are 12 x 12 or 12 x 24.

Use spray adhesive and cover the mat leaving a border so the glue doesn't get on the rollers or just spray the card stock's back to adhere to the makeshift mat.

Load and unload

When you load the mat into the Explore always make sure that it's up against the roller wheels and under the guides. This assures the material will load straight when you press the load button.

When the cut is complete never pull the mat out of the machine as this can damage the wheels. Always hit the unload button and then remove the mat.

To extend the life of the mat turn it around and load it from the bottom edge. Position the images on different parts of the mat instead of always cutting in the upper left corner .

Curling

Here's how to avoid curling material into a useless mess. When working with new mats they tend to hold on for dear life.

When you're pulling a project off the mat, do not remove the paper (or whatever material) up and away from the mat. This will cause it to curl into a mess.

Instead turn the mat over and curl it downward. Pull the rug away from the paper instead of pulling the form up and away from the mat.

It seems like a slight difference, but it will save you from trying to uncurl and flatten a project. Just remember how curled the mat was when you first unboxed it had to wait till it flattened out.

Blades

When cutting adhesive material, glue accumulates on the blades and should be periodically removed. Dip a Q-Tip in nail polish remover to clean any sticky residue build up. Check the cutting edge for nicks and that the tip is still intact .

Note: These blades are incredibly sharp. Always use the utmost care when removing them or replacing them into your Cricut. Never leave them lying within reach of children. Save the tips and cap the blades before trashing them.

For best results use the German Carbide blades. The regular Cricut blades will fit in the Explore blade housing even though they're shaped differently.

At this time there is no German Carbide deep cut blade for the Explore. The blade that comes with the deep cut housing for the Explore is the regular deep cutting blade.

Materials

When you're planning a project with a new material it's good to do a small test first to make sure the material cuts the way you want. This will save you from potential problems and from wasting a large amount of material.

Try one of the in-between settings on the Smart Set Dial. Some card stock is thicker than other types so you may need to adjust settings, use the multi cut settings or re-cut the image manually by hitting the cut button again.

By default, the Smart Set dial for paper, vinyl, iron-on, card stock, fabric, poster board has been set up to work best with Cricut products. Each material has three settings on the dial. If the cuts aren't deep enough, increase the pressure or decrease the pressure if the cuts are too deep. For even more control use the custom settings within Design Space.

Additionally, using a deep cutting blade (with the housing) or adjusting the mat's stickiness may help.

Iron-on Vinyl

Sometimes the iron-on vinyl sticks to the iron. First, be sure your iron is not too hot. Follow the recommendations on the product. Ensure you purchased the type of vinyl that can be applied with an iron not a professional heat press.

Next, try using parchment paper, Teflon sheet or a piece of cotton fabric between the vinyl and the iron. Use a firm heat resistant surface such as a ceramic tile or wooden cutting board to place your project on. Press and hold instead or ironing back and forth .

Always flip the image in Design Space. Put the vinyl shiny side down while cutting and shiny side up when attaching to the material.

Iron-on Glitter Vinyl

When working with glitter vinyl I move the dial one notch passed iron-on vinyl toward light card stock. It seems to cut better using that setting.

After you make the first cut do not remove the mat from the machine. Check to see if it cut through the vinyl, sometimes I have to run it through one more time for a complete cut. Especially if it's a new brand I haven't worked with.

Stencils

There are many materials you can use to make stencils. Some users suggested plastic file folders that can be found cheaply at a Dollar Store. Another option is sending laminating sheets through a laminating machine and then putting them through your Cricut to cut the stencil. Run it through twice to make sure cuts are complete .

Problems with machine pausing

If your Cricut machine stops while cutting, writing or scoring I've already made several suggestions to correct the problem here's another option.

It maybe the project itself if it always happens try deleting that project and recreating it. Turn off your computer and disconnect from your machine. Turn off your Cricut machine and wait a few moments. Then restart and reconnect.

Problems with Bluetooth wireless

If you're using an Explore Air or Explore Air 2 your Cricut machine is already Bluetooth enabled. But with an Explore or Explore One you will need to buy a Bluetooth adaptor.

When using Bluetooth be sure your machine is within nearby, no more than 15 feet from of the computer.

Make sure to verify your computer is Bluetooth enabled. If not, you'll need to buy a Bluetooth Dongle and place it in an unused USB port.

If you lose the Bluetooth connection, try uninstalling your Cricut under Bluetooth devices and then reinstalling .

Some people find their Design Space software works faster using the USB cord instead of the Bluetooth connection.

Chapter 5: FAQs about the Cricut Explore Air 2

Why does Design Space say my Cricut machine is already in use when it's not?

To resolve this, make sure that you've completed the New Machine Setup for your Cricut. Try Design Space in another browser. The two that work best are Google Chrome and Mozilla Firefox; if it doesn't work in one of those, try the other. If that doesn't clear the error, try a different USB port and USB cable. Disconnect the machine from the computer and turn it off. While it's off, restart your computer. After your computer restarts, reconnect the machine and turn it on. Wait a few moments, then try Design Space again. If you're still having the same problem, contact Cricut Member Care.

Why doesn't my cut match the preview in Design Space?

Test another image and see if the same thing happens. If it's only happening with the one project, create a new project and start over or try a different image. If it happens with a second project, and your machine is connected with Bluetooth, disconnect that and plug it in with a USB cable. Larger projects may sometimes have difficulty communicating the cuts over Bluetooth. If you can't connect with USB or the problem is still occurring, check that your computer matches or exceeds the system requirements for running Design Space. If it doesn't, try the project on a different computer or mobile device that does. If your computer does meet the requirements, open Design Space in a different browser and try again. If the problem continues, try a different USB cable. Finally, if the issue still hasn't resolved, contact Cricut Member Care.

What do I do if I need to install USB drivers for my Cricut machine?

Typically, the Cricut drivers are automatically installed when you connect it with a USB cable. If Design Space doesn't see your machine, you can try this to troubleshoot the driver installation. First, open Device Manager on your computer. You'll need to have administrator rights. For Windows 7, click Start, right-click on Computer, and select Manage. For Windows 8 and up, right-click on the Start icon and click Computer Management. Within Computer Management, click Device Manager on the left-hand side. Find your Cricut machine on the list—it should be listed under Ports. Still, it might be under Other Devices or Universal Serial Bus Controllers. Right-click on it and select Update Driver Software. In the box that pops up, select Browse My Computer. In the box on the next screen, type in %APPDATA% and click Browse. Another box will pop up where you can search through folders. Find AppData and expand it. Click Roaming, then CricutDesignSpace, then Web, then Drivers, then CricutDrivers, and click OK. Click Next to install these drivers. Once it's finished, restart your computer. Once it's on, open Design Space again to see if it recognizes your machine.

Why does my Cricut Maker say the blade is not detected?

Ensure that the tool in Clamp B is the same one Design Space recommends in the Load Tools step of the Project Preview screen. If you don't have that recommended tool, unload your mat and select Edit Tools on the Project Preview screen. Here, you can choose a different device. If the agency and the selection already match, carefully remove the device from Clamp B and clean the reflective band on the housing. Reinstall it in the clamp and press the Go button. If that doesn't resolve the problem, remove the tool again and clean the machine's sensor. Reinstall the tool and press Go again. If the Maker still doesn't detect the blade, try a simple test using a basic shape with one of the other tools. If that works, there may be something wrong with the drive housing of the original device. If the problem continues with other tools or don't have another tool to test, try uninstalling and reinstalling Design Space and retry your project. If the issue persists, or if you've discovered it's an issue with the tool housing, contact Cricut Member Care.

Is Wireless Bluetooth Adapter required for All Cricut Explore machines?

No. It is only required for Explore and Explore One. Explore Air and Explore Air 2 have in-built Bluetooth and therefore no need for Wireless Bluetooth Adapter .

How do you differentiate between the Cricut Explore machines?

The tool holder is the first difference. Explore One has one tool holder which means it can cut & score in two steps while Explore, Explore Air, and Explore Air 2 come with double tool holder for cut & write or cut & score in one single step.

Explore and Explore One require a Cricut Wireless Bluetooth Adapter to cut wirelessly from your iOS, Android or computer while Explore Air and Explore Air 2 have in-built Bluetooth.

Is carry bag included in Explore series machine package?

No. carry bag is not included in the package, but you can buy it separately.

Is it possible to write & score with my Explore One machine?

Yes, but to do this, you will need to buy Explore One Accessory Adapter. Switch this adapter with the blade housing to write or score with Explore One machine .

Are the weights and dimensions of Explore Series machine similar? What are their dimensions?

Yes, they are similar. The approximate weight is 9.5 kg (21 lbs), length: 56.33cm (22.17"), width: 17.76cm (6.99") and height: 15.16cm (5.97").

Why is my Cricut machine making a grinding noise?

If it's the carriage car making a loud noise after you press the cut button, and it sounds like the carriage might be hitting the side of the machine, record a short video of it and send it to Cricut Member Care. If the noise is coming from a brand-new engine the first time you use it, contact Cricut Member Care. Otherwise, make sure that you're using the original power cord that came with your device. If the machine isn't getting the correct voltage, it may produce a grinding sound. If you are using the machine's power cord, adjust your pressure settings. If it's too high, it might have an unusual sound. Decrease it in increments of 2–4, and do some test cuts. If it's still making the issue even after decreasing the cutting pressure, contact Cricut Member Care .

What if my Cricut is making a different loud noise?

Make sure that you don't have Fast Mode engaged for cutting or writing. If it's not on, take a short video of the problem to send to Cricut Member Care.

Why is my mat going into the machine crooked?

Check the roller bar to see if it's loose, damaged, or uneven. If it is, take a photo or video of it to send to Cricut Member Care. If the roller bar seems fine, make sure that you're using the right mat size for the machine. Next, make sure the mat is correctly lined up with the guides and that the edge is underneath the roller bar when you prepare to load it. If it's still loading crookedly even when properly lined up with the guides, try applying gentle pressure to the mat to get it under the roller bar once it starts. If none of this works, contact Cricut Member Care .

Why isn't the Smart Set Dial changing the material in Design Space?

Make sure that the USB cable between the computer and the Cricut

Explore is appropriately connected. If so, disconnect the Explorer from the computer and turn it off. Restart your computer. Once it's on, turn on the Explore, plug it into the computer, and try the cut again. If it still isn't changing the material, connect the USB cable to a different port on the computer. If it's still not working, try Design Space in multiple web browsers and see if the problem replicates. If it does, try an entirely different USB cable. Check for Firmware Updates for the Explore. If you don't have another USB cable, the Firmware Update doesn't help, or there are no Firmware Updates, contact Cricut Member Care.

What do I do if my Cricut Maker stopped partway through a cut?

If the Knife Blade stops cutting and the Go button is flashing, the Maker has encountered some sort of error. In Design Space, you'll get a notification that the blade is stuck. This might have been caused by the edge running into something like a knot or seam if too much dust or debris built up in the cut area or if the blade got into a gouge in the mat from a previous cut. To resume your project, do not unload the mat. This will lose your place in the project, and it will be impossible to get it lined up again. Check the cut area for dust or debris, and gently clean it. If there's dust on top of Clamp B, brush it off with a clean, dry paintbrush. Do not remove the blade. Once the debris is gone, press the Go button. The machine will take a moment to sense the Knife Blade again, and then it will resume cutting.

Why is my fabric getting caught under the rollers?

Be sure to cut down any fabric so that it fits on your mat without going past the adhesive. If you have stuck the fabric and realize it's hanging past the adhesive, use a ruler and a sharp blade to trim it. Or, if it's the correct size but slightly askew, unstick it and reposition it .

Why would my Cricut Maker continuously turn off during cuts?

This can happen from a build-up of static electricity while cutting foil and metal sheets. Makers in dry areas are more susceptible to this. Spritzing water in the air will dissipate the build-up. Be careful not to spray any water directly on the Maker. Using a humidifier or vaporizer in the area where you use your Maker can help avoid the static build-ups. If this doesn't seem to be what's causing the issue, contact Cricut Member Care.

What do I do about a failing or incomplete firmware update?

Be sure to use a computer to install the firmware update and that you're connected with a USB cable rather than Bluetooth. Verify that the computer meets the minimum system requirements; if it doesn't, you'll need to use another computer that does. If it does and you're still having problems, disconnect the Cricut from your computer and turn it off. Restart the computer. Once it's back on, open Design Space and try the firmware update again. If it still freezes up or doesn't complete, try the update using a different web browser. The next step is to try another USB cable. If that doesn't help or don't have another USB cable to try, contact Cricut Member Care.

What do I do if my Cricut machine is having power issues?

If your Cricut Maker, Cricut Explore One, or Cricut Explore Air 2 is having power issues, these are the troubleshooting steps. If the machine doesn't have any control or only has it sometimes, make sure that the plug is completely plugged into the power port on the device, the power adapter, and the wall outlet. The cutting mat can sometimes knock the power cable loose as it goes through the machine. You can avoid this by making sure the excess cord isn't bundled up behind the machine. If everything is securely plugged in, make sure that you're using the genuine Cricut power cable that came with your device and that the green light on the adapter is lit up. If you're not using the Cricut power cable, you can buy one or contact Cricut Member Care. If you are, try using a different wall outlet. If it's still having problems, try another Cricut power cable. If the issues continue even after this, take a short video of the issue happening and forward it to Cricut Member Care .

What do I do if I'm having issues with the machine's door?

If the door won't open or won't stay open, take a short video to forward on to Cricut Member Care. If the door won't close or won't stay closed, make sure there aren't any accessories loaded into the accessory clamp. If there aren't, take a photo or short video to forward to the Cricut Member Care team.

Where Can I Download Software for my Cricut Explore Air Machine?

For iOS users or Android users, you can get Cricut Design Space on the iOS App Store and Google Play, respectively. All you need do is to download it, install it and log in

For uses on a computer, visit design.cricut.com and then sign in with your login details. There will be a prompt to download Cricut Design Space. Download the plugin and install it and you are good to go .

Does My Cricut Explore Air need a Wireless Bluetooth Adapter?

No. Your machine is Bluetooth enabled. There is no need for a wireless Bluetooth adapter.

Can I link my cartridges to more than one account?

No. You can link your cartridges to only one Cricut account.

Can a cartridge be unlinked after it has been linked?

No. A cartridge once linked to an account cannot be unlinked.

I linked my cartridge to older software; can I still use it in Cricut Design Space?

Once you have linked your cartridges to older software like Cricut Craft Room, there will be no need to relink them on Cricut Design Space because they will be automatically available there .

I have linked my cartridges; how do I access them?

All the cartridges you have linked to your account can be found in your Cricut account. Go to Cricut Design Space and look under "My Image Sets" in the Insert Images window. You will find all the cartridges you have linked to your account.

Can I use physical cartridges without linking them?

No. For you to use any cartridge on your Cricut Explore Air, it must be linked to your account.

What type of materials can I cut with my cricut?

This machine cut more than 80 types of materials, clipboard, soda cans and even more thicker materials.

Can I upload my images?

You can upload your image or any other files that are already formatted and compatible with Cricut design space. The SVGs is one of the best image files because it uses 37 math formulas to create image based on point between lines.

What is the duration of my cutting mat?

You can cut through each cutting mat 20-50 full cut, but it depends on the card stack's nature and the cut size.

Can I make use of other paper size?

Yes, you can? One corner of the paper can just be aligning with the mat before loading your mat. Use the blade navigation button to adjust the cutting blade to the paper upper right side.

After which you tap on set paper size on your keypad, then allow the machine to start cutting on your paper

Can I learn how to create my own customize project with cricut design software without much stress?

yes, you can create and design your custom project any way you wish it to be without much weight.

Chapter 6: Tips for beginners

Want to enjoy your machine? Here are a few tips and tricks that will help you:

De-tack your cutting mat!

Your Cricut Explore Air will arrive with a cutting mat upon which you will put your projects before cutting. When purchased newly the cutting mat is usually very sticky. I would advise that you prime the cutting mat before your first use. Priming makes it less sticky such that your paper projects do not get damaged. You prime the cutting mat by placing a clean dry fabric over the cutting stock over the cutting mat and pulling it out again.

Keep Your Cutting Mat Clean

Use wipes to keep your cutting mat clean. Be careful with alcohol wipes as they could make the carpet lose stickiness. You can also use the plastic cover to store your cutting mat when it is not in use .

Use the Proper Tools

Use the correct Cricut Tools. The best tools are the tools from the Cricut Tool Set. This toolset contains tweezers, scrapers, scissors, spatula, and a weeding tool. These tools make work go very smoothly.

Start Your Cricut Journey with the Sample Project

It is best to start with the sample project and the material provided. The materials you will find in the package will be sufficient for you to start an initial sample project. Start with a simple sample project to have a feel of how the machine works.

Always Test Cuts

When carrying out projects, it is advisable to do a test cut before running the whole project. You can designate a simple cut to test run your settings before cutting material for the project. If the blade is not well set the test cut will reveal it .

Replace Pen Lids after Use

Replace the pen lids when you are done using your pens. This avoids it from drying out. It is a good thing that Design Space sends a notification that reminds you to put the lid back on!

Link Your Old Cricut Cartridges

If you have cartridges you have used with your older machines, you can still hook them up with your new device.

Bend the Cutting Mat to Get Materials off the Cutting Mat

To remove cut materials from the cutting mat (incredibly delicate Vinyl); you can bend the carpet away from the fabric. That way, you can use the spatula to help get the cut material off the cutting mat .

Use the Deep Cut Blade for Thicker Materials

Use the deep cut blade to cut through thick materials. These materials could be leather, cardboard or even chipboard. Get the edge and the blade housing.

Always replace the pen lids after use

You should ensure you avoid forgetting your pen in the machine after you are done with a project. This might result in your cell drying out, so you should always remember to have the lid back on it after you are done.

Linking your old Cricut Cartridges to your Design Space Account

In a situation where you have old cartridges from previous machines, it helps hook this up with your new machine. It is to be noted that cartridges can only be linked once. In a situation where you are buying a second-hand cartridge, you will need to confirm if it has not been linked to a machine before.

Get materials off the Cutting mat

Getting the project peeled from the mat can cause curling; therefore, you can instead just peel the mat from the project. Just have the carpet bent away from the card rather than the other way round.

Get the Deep Cut blade

You are advised to order the deep cut blade. It is useful in cutting through thick cards, chipboard, leather, etc. It works perfectly with the Cricut Explore Air 2.

You should get the blade housing along with the blade.

Always Replace the Blades

It is usual for Cricut blades to wear out after being used for sometimes. The blade will start to be ineffective and will no longer be smooth; at this point, it is necessary to have the blades changed. Some other signs that show that it's time for the blade to be replaced include when it starts lifting or pulling the vinyl off the backing seat, they start to tear the cards or vinyl and incomplete cutting process.

Keep Your Cutting Mat Clean

Use wipes to keep your cutting mat clean. Be careful with alcohol wipes as they could make the carpet lose stickiness. You can also use the plastic cover to store your cutting mat when it is not in use.

Use the Proper Tools

Use the correct Cricut Tools. The best tools are the tools from the Cricut Tool Set. This toolset contains tweezers, scrapers, scissors, spatula, and a weeding tool. These tools make work go very smoothly .

Start Your Cricut Journey with the Sample Project

It is best to start with the sample project and the material provided. The materials you will find in the package will be sufficient for you to create an initial sample project. Start with a simple sample project to have a feel of how the machine works.

Always Test Cuts

When carrying out projects, it is advisable to do a test cut before running the whole project. You can designate a simple amount to test run your settings before cutting material for the project. If the blade is not well set the test cut will reveal it.

Replace Pen Lids after Use

Replace the pen lids when you are done using your pens. This avoids it from drying out. It's a good thing that Design Space sends a notification that reminds you to put the lid back on !

Link Your Old Cricut Cartridges

If you have cartridges you have used with your older machines, you can still hook them up with your new machine.

Bend the Cutting Mat to Get Materials off the Cutting Mat

To remove cut materials from the cutting mat (especially delicate Vinyl); you can bend the mat away from the material. That way, you can use the spatula to help get the cut material off the cutting mat.

Use the Deep Cut Blade for Thicker Materials

Use the deep cut blade to cut through thick materials. These materials could be leather, cardboard or even chipboard. Get the blade and the blade housing .

Use Different Pens Where Necessary

Like you should use different blades for different materials; you should use different pens for different uses. There are different pen adapters available which you can use with your machine.

Make Use of Free Fonts

There are many free fonts you can use. You can make use of these fonts for free instead of purchasing fonts on Cricut Access. When you identify a desired free front, download it and install it on your computer. The font will appear on Cricut Design Space.

Use Different Blades for Different Materials

Do not use one single blade for all the different materials you will cut. For example, you can have one blade for cardboard, another for only leather and one for vinyl. It is best to have different blades for different materials because each material wears differently on the blade. A dedicated blade will be best because it will be tuned to the peculiarities of each material.

Use Weeding Boxes for Intricate Patterns

When cutting delicate or intricate patterns it is important to use weeding boxes in the process. Create a square or rectangle using the square tool in Cricut Design Space and place it such that all your design elements are all in it. Doing this makes weeding easier as all your design elements are grouped within the square or rectangle you have created.

Always Remember to Set the Dial

This sounds like stating the obvious setting the dial to the right material is something you can easily forget. The consequences of forgetting to set the dial to the appropriate material range from damaged cutting mats to shallow cuts on the materials. You can prevent these by always setting the dial before cutting .

Make use of the Free SVG files

Apart from making use of the designs available in the Design Space store, you can have your SVG files created or employ other SVG files available on the internet. This will help you in saving a lot of money.

Other pens compatible with the Cricut Explore Air 2

Apart from the Cricut pens, we have other pens that are compatible with the Cricut Explore Air 2 machine and any other machine that uses the accessory adapter. These pens include American craft pens and Sharpie pens. Nevertheless, the Cricut pens, when compared to

these other pens, are of higher quality.

HAVE THE MAT CORRECTLY LOADED

Before beginning the cutting process, it is crucial to ensure that your mat is successfully loaded. You have to ensure that it slips correctly under the rollers.

In a situation where the mat is not correctly loaded, the machine may just start cutting before the grid top on the mat or may not cut at all.

Tips on How to Do Iron-On or Heat Transfer Vinyl Project

A heat transfer vinyl has a clear plastic back that allows it to adhere to fabrics when applied to it. Therefore, iron-on vinyl project is a great way to create your customized t-shirts, hats, bags, totes and more. You can use the Cricut Maker to cut the vinyl material and then do the heat transfer vinyl project yourself. This is an amazing way to be classy and creative. Here are tips on how to iron-on a vinyl project :

Prepare the project area and measure it correctly. There is no need for assumptions as this may prove costly later on. So, get a tape to measure the length and width of your vinyl material. Ensure that you use the same tape to measure all your project materials; this is very important.

Adhere strictly to the manufacturer's instructions and recommendations for your iron-on vinyl material. This will save you a lot of time and reduce waste which will result from doing the wrong procedure.

Ensure that you mirror your image before cutting. Mirroring the image refers to flip it so that it can cut backwards. Though, a pop up may remind you to mirror the image if you have not done so. Mirroring the image will make sure that the heat transfer side of the image will appear correctly on the shirt or bag.

Place the iron-on vinyl on the mat with liner side down. The right mat for this project is Cricut Standard Grip Cutting Mat.

Place any thin cotton material between your vinyl project and the pressing iron to avoid melting the vinyl material.

Use heat press to heat transfer vinyl to your project. This method will ensure that the right pressure and temperature is applied to the vinyl for bonding between the it and project. This is the recommended method but if you don't have a heat press, then make sure that your pressing iron does not go higher than is required for the fabric you are using. Then, press the iron firmly on the cotton material covering the vinyl project.

Peel the liner off the vinyl. If some of the vinyl pieces are not firmly attached, put the cotton material back over it and again apply pressure on it with the iron. Do this at short intervals until you meet your aim.

Note that heat transfer should be applied only to fabrics or solids that can withstand the heat from the iron.

These same steps are also applied when you create Christmas tea towels and other customized iron-on vinyl on fabrics. If there are steps you didn't get quite well, do well to go over and read them again. As you grab the content, allow your creative mind to roam and discover ways to beautify this design to come up with your customized design .

There are many designs that you already have, and you are eager to try your hands. Do not be afraid, just get busy and with the above steps to guide you, there is no problem.

Free fonts are available for your project

Many free fonts are available, which can be used for your different projects. You can visit the fontbundles.net to get fonts downloaded. After downloading, install it on your computer. It should then automatically appear on your Cricut Design Space.

Installation of Fonts into the Design Space

You will need to sign out of your Cricut Design space and sign in back into it after you have successfully installed the fonts on your computer to have the new fonts show up in the Design space. In some cases, you may also need to restart your computer to have the font show up.

What to do when the Cutting mat begins to lose its stick the cutting mats always come sticky; it is, therefore, important to always clean the mat to ensure they maintain this stickiness for a longer time.

When the cutting mat has eventually lost their stickiness, and you don't have a new one to get them replaced yet, you can make use of tape in holding down your vinyl or card in place while avoiding areas that will need to be cut.

Recommended for taping down your card or vinyl when the cutting mat loses its stickiness is the medium tack painters' tape.

Making use of different blades for different materials

Having dedicated blades for different materials is a way of keeping the sharpness of the blades intact and doing an excellent cutting job. For example, having a blade to be used on vinyl only while another for cardstock, helps in having your blade around for such a long time simply because different materials will wear differently on your blades. Vinyl is more easily cut on the blade than when cutting through a card.

- Always Mirror your image when cutting HTV

IT IS STILL ADVISABLE TO GET YOUR IMAGE MIRRORED WHEN CUTTING the HTV. For example, when cutting heat transfer vinyl using your Cricut, there will be a need to get your designed mirrored .

Once you have selected the "Make it" option, you will be prompted with an opportunity to mirror your design, which will have to be chosen for each mat.

Have your HTV placed on the Cutting Mat the right way in the upward direction You will have to put your vinyl shiny side facing down on the cutting mat to cut the heat transfer vinyl so that that carrier sheet will appear underneath with the dull vinyl side placed on the top.

- Always remember to set the dial

IT IS EASY TO FORGET HAVING THE MATERIAL SETTING CHANGED MOST TIMES, especially when you are done designing and want to start the cutting process. Though the Cricut Design Space will always let you know what material you have the dial set to as you are about to get a design cut out, this can be overlooked as well. To save yourself any mistake of cutting through immediately after your design is done with, you are always advised to have your dial settings checked .

- Use Different Pens Where Necessary

JUST LIKE YOU USE SHOULD USE DIFFERENT BLADES FOR DIFFERENT MATERIALS; you should use different pens for different uses. There are different pen adapters available which you can use with your machine.

Make Use of Free Fonts

There are many free fonts you can use. You can make use of these fonts for free instead of purchasing fonts on Cricut Access. When you identify a desired free front, download it, and install it on your computer. The font will appear on Cricut Design Space.

- Use Different Blades for Different Materials

DO NOT USE ONE SINGLE BLADE FOR ALL THE DIFFERENT MATERIALS you will cut. For example, you can have one blade for cardboard, another for only leather and one for vinyl. It is best to have different blades for different materials because each material wears differently on the blade. A dedicated blade will be best because it will be tuned to the peculiarities of each material.

- Use Weeding Boxes for Intricate Patterns

WHEN CUTTING DELICATE OR INTRICATE PATTERNS IT IS IMPORTANT TO USE WEEDING BOXES IN THE PROCESS. Create a square or rectangle using the square tool in Cricut Design Space and place it such that all your design elements are all in it. Doing this makes weeding easier as all your design elements are grouped within the square or rectangle you have created.

- Always Remember to Set the Dial

THIS SOUNDS LIKE STATING THE OBVIOUS SETTING THE DIAL TO THE right material is something you can easily forget. The consequences of forgetting to set the dial to the appropriate material range from damaged cutting mats to shallow cuts on the materials. You can prevent these by always setting the dial before cutting.

Additional tips on Effective Use of Your Cricut Explore Air 2

Always clean your Cricut cutting mat after every project. Roll a lint roller over the Cricut mat to remove tiny leftovers of dirt and lint from the surface of the mat.

To make absolutely sure that you do not regret your action while using any Cricut machine, Cricut Explore Air 2 included, make it a habit of always testing the cutting of your material by using a small piece of the material you wish to cut first before cutting the main material. Watch out these materials: wood, fabric, or felt because present different challenges during the cut process.

When you want to detach your processed material from the cutting mat after unloading it, roll the Cricut mat backwards away from the material instead of peeling the material away from the Cricut mat.

Always organize your blades and knifes in separate compartment or container. This will help you pick the correct blade or knife for a particular project because mixing them up may lead you to use an inappropriate blade for a project which might result to blunting the blades or even outright damage.

Organize your Cricut tools so that they will not be flying everywhere around the project area to avoid messing up with your project or even causing you bodily harm. These tools include scissors, spatula, scoring tools, pic, weeding tools, etc.

It is important that you keep your blades sharp every time so that you do not get your materials messed up while cutting and get them replaced when necessary .

Make sure that you dispose of the used ones properly to avoid injury to you and those around you especially moms with little kids. I am sure you do not want your kids to get hurt from the blades.

Use this important resource from the makers of Cricut Explore Air 2; their website Cricut.com where you are granted access to many YouTube videos and project ideas. If you need more help, search for information on Google or Pinterest.

Using features such as fonts and a few projects on Cricut will cost you a few bucks but you can cut this cost by subscribing to Cricut Access.

With this, there is worry of cartridges and all purchases will stay in your account.

If the cut edges of the material, you are working on, is rough and uneven then it simply means that the blade you are using is blunt. The solution is to replace the blade with another one.

If the material, on the cutting mat, is moving while being cut, then it means that your mat is not sticky enough. The solution is to replace your mat and the used material or use tape to hold your material firmly to the mat.

Conclusion

I believe that you have gained insight into the possibilities associated with Cricut Explore Air 2 machine, increased your knowledge about it and obtained value for money spent in purchasing this book.

Presently your innovative potential is exponential. Cricut explore air 2 offers the most stretched out scope of tools for cutting, scoring, composing, and including enlivening impacts – all so you can take on any undertaking, you can envision. Besides, with more devices coming, Cricut Maker develops with you as you ace each new craft. Choose a wide assortment of sewing examples and quilt squares, including hundreds from Simplicity. Cricut Maker cuts and denotes every one of your pieces in only a couple of clicks .

This book will sure help your creative ability in the world of craft, and you will be amazed how much people appreciate the good things you will be creating with your Cricut Explore Air 2 machine. Take your place in the world of art after reading and digesting this book to start creating beautiful craft for yourself, family and friends.

CPSIA information can be obtained
at www.ICGtesting.com
Printed in the USA
BVHW090552090621
609011BV00011B/2152